Storytelling
Professionally

STORYTELLING PROFESSIONALLY

The
Nuts and Bolts
of a
Working Performer

HARLYNNE GEISLER

1997
LIBRARIES UNLIMITED, INC.
Englewood, Colorado

LIBRARIES UNLIMITED, INC.
P.O. Box 6633
Englewood, CO 80155-6633
1-800-237-6124

Production Editor: Kevin W. Perizzolo
Copy Editor: Tama Serfoss
Proofreader: Jason Cook
Indexer: Nancy Fulton
Typesetter: Kay Minnis

Library of Congress Cataloging-in-Publication Data

Geisler, Harlynne, 1950-
    Storytelling professionally : the nuts and bolts of a working
performer / Harlynne Geisler.
      xviii, 151 p. 22x25 cm.
      Includes bibliographical references and index.
      ISBN 1-56308-370-1
      1. Storytelling. 2. Folklore--Performance. 3. Storytellers--
Vocational guidance. I. Title.
GR72.3.G45   1997
808.5'43--dc20   96-41964
                                      CIP

This book is dedicated to the memory of two important people:

> Minnie Geisler, my grandmother, who gave me just a little of her boundless energy, and Warren Barnes, my husband's grandfather, who showed me that storytelling in the family circle is still alive if we have the patience to listen.

It is also dedicated to those who have supported me emotionally during all my years of professional storytelling: my ever-loving husband, Judson Farrar; the women of my retreat; and my friends Suzi, Darrel, and Caitlin Westmoreland.

Contents

Part 2—Tapping the Markets

Part 4—Situations Requiring Special Attention

Introduction

From Librarian to Performer:
My Story

I have always loved acting. One of my earliest memories is of playing Rachel, who lets her seven beloved sons die rather than deny their God, at my temple. My sixth-grade boyfriend cast me in the role of Cleopatra in his version of Caesar's death. Whenever possible, I played a haughty Indian princess in childhood games.

I have always been an avid reader. Neighbors would warn my mother that I would be hit by a car if I didn't look up from my book as I crossed the street. I read at every opportunity. "Take your nose out of that book," my mother would order. Instead, I would hide under the covers with a flashlight and read long after the lights went out.

While in college in 1970 I joined a guerrilla theater troupe. We would take over public spaces to put on plays about the importance of peace. I was the only one who bothered to memorize my lines.

After earning my master's degree in library science from the University of Illinois, I spent two years as a public school librarian. Then I moved to San Diego and became a librarian at a private school for five years. However, being a librarian didn't seem to be the right career for me. I hated faculty meetings and felt restricted and unable to exercise my creativity. To be comfortable, I would wear long, flowing skirts to work and kick off my shoes—then I would wander around the library looking for them. As a way to be creative, I started taking drama courses at night and continued with a private drama coach.

I was bit by the storytelling bug at a state library conference when I saw a performance by Carol Birch, a former librarian and a nationally known storyteller. In one tale she had me hooked. Here was the perfect way to combine my love of books and drama. I took courses in storytelling from Birch and others, read every book I could get my hands on, helped found a local storytelling group, started a newsletter, and attended a variety of storytelling conferences (even during my honeymoon!).

At the same time I was powerfully affected by Bruno Bettelheim's book, *The Uses of Enchantment: The Meaning and Importance of Fairy Tales*, in which he says, "Without fantasy to give us hope, we do not have the strength to meet the adversities of life." Helping children survive the many traumas of growing up was vital to me, and storytelling and story listening seemed to be avenues for healing. I told stories to children of every age and practiced on adults by donating my services to local clubs and churches.

Finally in 1980, at the age of 30, I resigned from the school where I worked to pursue storytelling professionally. I used my retirement money as a nest egg. I also accepted a part-time job as a public librarian so I would have some stable income while I built up my client list.

Pursuing my career as a storyteller often led me to difficult choices. When the director of the public library refused to let me reschedule one day of work so that I could audition for a gig as a bookstore storyteller, I resigned and took a job for a different library system as a substitute librarian. Eventually, it paid off. After eight years as a part-time public librarian, I became a full-time freelance storyteller.

My friends were concerned. "You're going to be a what?" they asked. "But how will you make a living?"

My first homemade brochure was bright yellow, with a cute dragon, the words "Old Stories for a New Age" on the cover, and an amateurish photograph of myself inside. I mailed it to every club listed in a reference work at the library and waited for them to call. They didn't. So I nerved myself to make calls and to send fliers to local schools and libraries. Slowly, the bookings started to come in. I established a niche telling and teaching storytelling at elementary schools. During the slow summer months I would live off my nest egg, replacing it during the busy Halloween and winter-holiday seasons.

Three years later, I was able to afford a professional to help me create my next brochure. He told me that my bright-yellow brochure with its cartoonish cover probably attracted children, but children do not hire entertainers; adults do. He helped me design a subdued, business-like, tan brochure more likely to appeal to prospective bookers. It did.

My friends were amazed. I was actually doing what so few of us dare to do—living my dream and succeeding. I made more money each year until the recession hit California. Then my earnings went down considerably. It was tough, but after toying with the idea of getting a regular job, I realized that I enjoyed being my own boss too much.

As I began to learn through experimentation what worked and what didn't, I wrote about my experiences as a professional storyteller in my own newsletter and in regular columns in the *California Traditional Music Society Journal* and *Laugh Makers Magazine*, an international periodical for professionals in the variety arts such as clowns, jugglers, ventriloquists, magicians, puppeteers, storytellers, and balloon artists. My articles have appeared in 25 other publications, including the *Alaskan Folklorian*, the *Jade Dragon* (California), the *Joyful Child Journal* (Arizona), *Story Art Magazine* (Ohio), *Telling Tales* (Australia), *Charlotte Folk Music Society Magazine* (North Carolina), and *Storytelling Magazine* (Tennessee).

Eventually, I changed the name of my newsletter from the *Storytellers of San Diego Newsletter* to *Story Bag Newsletter*. When I realized that 80 percent of my subscribers were outside San Diego, I changed the name again to *Story Bag: A National Storytelling Newsletter* and also became the managing editor of the *Texas Teller* newsletter for two years. My first book was *The Best of the Story Bag: 32 Articles and Stories from the Story Bag Newsletter.*

Over the years, I have taught storytelling to clowns, magicians, teachers, children, college students, parents, puppeteers, librarians, ministers, and storytellers in New York, Texas, Illinois, Arizona, New Mexico, and California. I have performed from Aurora, New York, to Alberta, Canada, to Austin, Texas, to Albuquerque, New Mexico, to Anaheim, California . . . and that's just the "A" list!

People from all over the country have asked me about such practical matters as how to handle contracts, where to find good stories for special programs, how to determine fees, and much more. I answered every question and started a column in *Story Bag* to share some of my answers. However, the same questions have come up so often that I finally decided to save my breath and write all the answers down in this book.

Not Always a Fairy Tale

Storytelling has always been a challenge as an art and as a business. For example, there are bad days, when . . .

- my contract request for the karaoke to be placed in a different room has been ignored, and the rock music starts blaring during my show;

- the substitute teacher is trying to get the eighth-graders to settle down so I can begin, and they ignore her;

- a child in the third row throws up, and I have to continue my assembly while the janitor sprinkles sawdust;

- the teacher leaves a message on my answering machine three days before my class at her school is to begin, telling me that my nine-week course has been canceled due to lack of funding; or

- a mother blurts out that for what I charge for a birthday party, she could take the kids to Chuck E. Cheese.

On these days I wonder if I shouldn't have remained a librarian with a pension plan, a regular paycheck, and business expenses from pencils to computers paid by my employer.

But then there are the good days, when . . .

- I walk into the room, and kids I saw last week tell each other, "It's the storyteller! Cool!" and cheer;

- a poet tells me my introduction to a folktale inspired her most healing poem;

- senior citizens who at first resented being treated like children, tell me how much they enjoyed my storytelling program;

- I see a third-grader at the back of the library open his mouth as I use my hands to create the water buffalo's open mouth, almost as if he's become a part of the fairy tale; or

- my research and imagination pays off, and I figure out a way to adapt an American folktale so it incorporates whales, dolphins, cookies, and participation, as the Girl Scout leaders requested.

On these days I know why I am a storyteller.

Using This Book

What's your story? Are you a school teacher who wants to earn extra income after retirement? Are you a public librarian dying to kick off your shoes and work for yourself? Are you an unpublished author who believes that your stories are worth hearing? Are you a clown who wants to make the leap from weekend birthday party gigs to full-time, professional clowning? Are you a magician who wishes to perform beyond your own town?

Although this book has the word *storytelling* in the title, what I have written applies to performers of all varieties—clowns, magicians, jugglers, ventriloquists, actors, mimes, singers, musicians, and so on. This book also provides advice to those performers who have full-time jobs in schools, libraries, hospitals, law firms, churches, and temples.

The Chinese have a saying: "Every journey begins with one step." By picking up this book, you have taken at least two steps on your road. You have decided storytelling is an art and a business you wish to learn more about, and you are investigating your options as a professional storyteller. I would like you to literally pat yourself on the back and tell yourself, out loud, "Good for me!" It's also going to be good for all your bookers and listeners.

If you have any questions or comments about the information contained in this book, please consider me an accessible resource. You may write me in care of *Story Bag: A National Storytelling Newsletter*, 5361 Javier Street, San Diego, CA 92117-3215, or call 619-569-9399 and leave a message. Please be sure to enclose a self-addressed, stamped envelope or give me permission to call you collect if you wish a reply. I am also available for lectures, workshops, and shows.

If you write or call any of the resources you find in this book, please tell them where you found the information. If you know of companies, books, tapes, or other resources (including those published after 1996) that should be included in future editions of this book, please send me complete information.

Further Reading

Bettelheim, Bruno. *The Uses of Enchantment: The Meaning and Importance of Fairy Tales*. New York: Vintage Books, 1976.

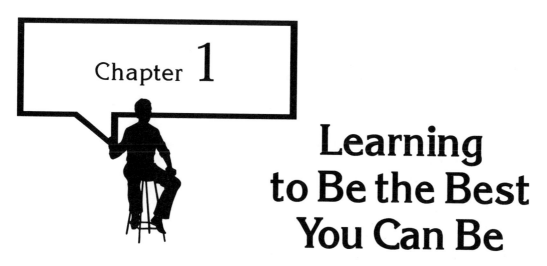

Chapter 1

Learning to Be the Best You Can Be

Drawing the Dragon

Many hundreds of years ago there was an emperor who lived in China. He had been born in the year of the dragon and had grown up loving dragons. The emperor had dragons embroidered on his silk robes. Every year he watched the dragon dancers with delight. He filled the Forbidden City where he lived with sculptures and paintings of dragons. Yet when the emperor looked at the dragons that surrounded him, none seemed quite right.

So the emperor tried to picture the perfect dragon. He thought and thought. Finally he saw in his mind's eye a perfect dragon. It had a long curving tail, five sharp claws on each paw, and a fierce expression on its scaly face. The emperor said to himself, "Surely one of my court artists can draw this wonderful dragon just as I see it." He called for all of his court artists and described the dragon to them in detail—down to the last claw.

All the court artists tried to draw the dragon as the emperor pictured it, but they all failed. The emperor proclaimed that whoever could draw the dragon would have his weight in gold—but whoever attempted and failed would have his eyes put out. There were still some painters who thought they could meet the challenge, but they soon stumbled away from the Forbidden City with empty eye sockets. All of China was whispering about the emperor's demand.

In a small hut outside the walled city lived a poor man who had been painting for many years. When he heard what the emperor wanted, he asked to be ushered into the emperor's presence. Once there, the artist said, "Son of Heaven, I think I can give you the picture you wish, but it will take me a year, and I must go far away from here."

"Whatever you like," said the emperor. "You may have exactly one year. However, in one year to the minute you must present me with the drawing, or I will have your head chopped off. And if the painting is not exactly right, you will lose your eyes as have the others who tried and failed." Given those words, some people could not believe that the young man left the room with a smile on his face.

1

No one saw the young artist for many months. When the year was almost up, the emperor prepared to send troops after the man—this arrogant fellow who must now be too frightened to return—and chop off his head.

But, with ten minutes of his year to spare, the young man finally appeared. He had a scroll of paper beneath one arm and he carried a bag with his tools.

The emperor was so eager to see the dragon he had dreamed of that he grabbed the scroll and unrolled it . . . then he stood, aghast, to see only a blank piece of paper.

The emperor was furious. "Do you toy with me? Do you consider me a fool?" He motioned to a guard, who began drawing his sword.

"No, Son of Heaven," replied the artist. "I still have ten minutes, and I only need five." And he took out his ink stick, ground part of it into his grinding stone, and mixed the powder with water in the indentation of the stone. He then dipped his bamboo brush into the ink and with a swiftness that was almost unbelievable began to draw. After five minutes he had produced an exquisite rendering of the exact beast that the emperor had been imagining.

The emperor was happy, but he was also puzzled. "I don't understand. You said it would take you a whole year, but you began and finished the picture in five minutes. Why didn't you draw it for me a year ago?"

"Because, Son of Heaven, it took me a year to learn to draw the dragon in five minutes," answered the young man.

The End 📖

This story was inspired by Chinese folklore. I wrote it to illustrate the hard work that lies behind what seems like effortless art.

What Is Storytelling?

Storytelling has been defined in many ways by many people. The Committee on Storytelling of the National Council of Teachers of English is made up of teachers who define it as follows:

Storytelling is relating a tale to one or more listeners through voice and gesture. It is not the same as reading a story aloud or reciting a piece from memory or acting out a drama—though it shares common characteristics with these arts. The storyteller looks into the eyes of the audience, and together they compose the tale. The storyteller begins to see and re-create, through voice and gesture, a series of mental images; the audience, from the first moment of listening, squints, stares, smiles, leans forward or falls asleep, letting the teller know whether to slow down, speed up, elaborate, or just finish. Each listener, as well as each teller, actually composes a unique set of story images derived from meanings associated with words, gestures, and sounds. The experience can be profound, exercising the thinking and touching the emotions of both teller and listener.[1]

Why Is Storytelling Important?

Stories inform us about other cultures, times, and peoples as well as about our own culture, time, and selves. Storytelling inspires the imagination, heals the soul, and challenges our beliefs. Storytelling is as much an outlet for the quiet person who tells haltingly of a past experience as for the accomplished ham who enjoys attracting every eye.

Where Do I Find the Time?

Americans are busy people. Well, that's not exactly a news flash to you! In our modern world everyone is rushing around and seeming to get less done. The fact that we can do things faster makes us believe that we *have* to. We've gone from buttons to zippers to Velcro, from books to television to videocassette recorders with remote controls. Instead of reading a book in the morning as I used to, now I watch the television programs I videotaped the night before, impatiently fast-forwarding through scenes that don't move quickly enough for me.

You've seen the effect of this speeding-up on the listeners in your audiences. They (and you) are less relaxed and more tired. Our bodies and minds cannot stand the modern pace. Something's got to give. We see it happening in others and can feel it internally.

Listening to stories helps slow down the world. I remember listening to a tape of tales told by Joe Hayes. I didn't like it because he spoke so slowly. If it had been a record, I would have been tempted to switch the turntable speed from $33\frac{1}{3}$ to 45 rpm. I just wanted him to get to the point.

Finally I had the chance to hear Joe in person. He spoke just as slowly, and the whole audience (including me) relaxed. Suddenly "the point" wasn't as important as the journey. We listeners felt nurtured and as if we had all the time in the world. This is because storytelling occurs in human time, a welcome reprieve from living in machine time.

Stories and Morality

When I enter classrooms to talk to the students, I often see posters that admonish children to be polite, kind, and generous. As any religious leader can tell you, moral messages are better conveyed by subtle stories than by strict lectures. Evil, rude, greedy characters often have their way early in a folktale or fairy tale—as in life—but goodness always wins out in the end. Many stories have a character sharing their last penny or crust of bread with an older or poorer person or helping someone in need. Later this character receives that kindness back just when it is needed most.

I have found in my experience that stories create trust and love within myself and my listeners. Joe Hayes believes that language takes the place of physical touching as children get older. Storytelling is a use of language that creates closeness. Joe finds that when he first enters a room filled with children, they look at him as a giant and are a little scared, but by his second story they're often climbing into his lap.

Storytelling is a gift you can give your listeners . . . and yourself.

Who Tells Stories?

People who tell stories professionally include ministers, librarians, rabbis, teachers, social workers, nurses, counselors, doctors, lawyers, parents, and sales representatives. Often these people would not describe themselves as "storytellers," but they use narratives to explain, teach, sell, preach, and persuade. Other tellers work for themselves and perform at hospitals, churches, temples, schools, libraries, business meetings, corporate training sessions, law conferences, family gatherings, and stores. Because most people think stories are just for children, most freelance performers work primarily in settings for children, but many also find themselves telling in adult venues.

Where Are Stories Told?

Stories are appropriate anywhere two or more people come together. Any setting can work (although some are better than others), no group is too small (though some can be too large), and the audience can be any age. A partial list of audiences, events, and places storytellers can explore follows. However, as long as this list is, it's only a start. You will probably think of a few more.

Audiences

- Boy Scouts and Girl Scouts
- Boys and Girls Clubs
- business associations
- clown clubs and other variety arts associations
- ecology groups (e.g., the Sierra Club)
- educational groups (e.g., Association for the Education of Young Children, parent-teacher organizations, etc.)
- ethnic associations
- feminist groups
- 4-H clubs
- historical associations
- nature interpreters groups
- library associations
- new age groups
- parent groups
- psychological groups
- senior citizen groups (e.g., the American Association of Retired Persons)
- social concerns groups
- special populations within a school or community (e.g., gifted students, the hearing-impaired, etc.)
- student associations
- teacher associations
- women's clubs (e.g., the American Association of University Women)

Events

- after-school programs
- banquets
- camp programs
- children's festivals
- religious gatherings
- community festivals
- conferences and conventions for any group
- corporation parties
- drama, education, literature, history, and speech classes
- educational conferences
- elderhostel classes
- ethnic and folk festivals
- fund-raisers
- holiday parties and programs
- International Reading Association conferences (state, local, and regional)
- International Whole Language Umbrella conferences (state, local, and regional)
- American Library Association conferences (state, local, and regional)
- luncheons
- park programs
- private parties (e.g., birthday parties, baby showers, retirement celebrations, etc.)
- puppet shows
- radio shows
- religious retreats
- renaissance festivals
- school district in-service days
- storytelling concert series
- storytelling festivals
- teaching conferences
- television programs
- variety shows

Places

- art galleries
- botanical gardens
- campgrounds
- churches
- coffeehouses
- colleges and universities
- homeless shelters
- hospitals
- hotels
- libraries (school, university, special, and public)
- museums (children's, art, etc.)
- preschools
- prisons
- private and public schools (elementary, junior high, and high school)
- recreation centers
- restaurants

- senior citizen centers and retirement homes
- shelters for abused women and children
- shopping centers and stores (book, toy, craft, new age, etc.)
- spas
- summer schools

- temples
- theaters
- YWCAs/YMCAs/YMHAs

To make a long list short, stories can be told just about anywhere, to any audience, for a wide variety of purposes: education, entertainment, and enlightenment.

Becoming a Storyteller

Not too long ago, I received a phone call from Richmond, Virginia. The woman calling said, "Everyone says that I'm a good talker and funny and that I should do something with that. I decided that storytelling would be the way to go. You're a professional storyteller. How do I go about it?"

The caller had never formally told a story before, so I suggested she begin by donating her services to different organizations. "But I want to do this for a living," she interrupted.

"Yes, but first you need to gain some experience and see what it is like to tell before different age groups. You can't expect people to pay you when you don't know what you're doing."

As we continued to talk, the caller asked me where she could find stories. I told her the public library was a good source, but then I warned her, "But be aware that if stories are copyrighted, you must get permission to tell them for money."

"What!?" The caller was beginning to realize that storytelling professionally wasn't going to as easy as sitting around the kitchen table making her family laugh. I was sorry to bring a dose of hard reality to her dream, but the call showed me once again that this book is needed.

Being a freelance storyteller requires a high level of commitment and effort. It also takes a person with special characteristics and one with plenty of emotional and financial support.

Personal Characteristics of Storytellers

Storytellers come in as wide a range of personalities as people in other fields. However, some traits they share are the ability to perform in front of a group, the ability to speak with authority and animation, a sense of caring about the audience and their needs, the discipline to work at storytelling as an art and as a business, the emotional strength to handle rejection, and the belief in their own talents and gifts.

Support Network

Storytellers just beginning professionally also need a strong support network. While financial support is helpful, try to find people who will support you emotionally and artistically. These can be storytellers and other performers or appreciative yet critical listeners on whom you can try out new stories or project ideas. They can be friends and family who are willing to listen to your horror stories without saying, "I told you it was a bad idea to become a storyteller" and who will break out the champagne when you want to boast about a success. Try joining storytelling clubs and associations where you can share and receive professional advice as well as emotional support.

Financial Resources

Before you take the final leap and become a full-time storyteller, be sure you consider certain hard financial facts. When you work for yourself, there is no benefits package. You don't get paid sick leave or holidays. You aren't covered by a company insurance or retirement plan. All office expenses, such as long distance phone calls and typing paper are going to come out of your pocket.

Look at your current expenses. Can you handle your basic expenses (the mortgage or rent, car loan, groceries, utilities, and so on)? Then calculate your new business expenses (business cards, brochures, stationery, fliers, new computer programs, costumes, signs, mailings, showcases, booths at conventions, etc.). Don't forget to figure in the cost of gas to drive to shows, maintenance on the car, extra phone expenses, stamps for mailings and correspondence, photocopies of handouts, a retirement plan, health insurance, and other essential business expenses. Can you cover all these expenses without going heavily into debt? Perhaps you should sit down with an accountant and make a budget. If you're lucky, you have a spouse or family member who can help support you or at least provide you with insurance and retirement coverage until you become established.

Keep a part-time job so that you have some money coming in as you build up your business. Save enough money to cover all your bills for three months so you can make it through the slow times. Whenever you have to dip into that savings, be sure you replace it as soon as you can. (See chapter 9 for more financial advice.)

Getting Started

It's usually easiest to begin telling stories to familiar audiences. Because I had been a school and public librarian, I decided to tell to children in schools and libraries. This was an easy sell because storytelling encourages reading, so teachers and librarians were happy to hire me as a storyteller. Many local librarians knew me and had heard me tell while I worked as a librarian. I asked them for advice on how to get hired. I sent out a flier listing my different shows with rave reviews from teachers and librarians. I didn't put a price on that first flier. When a teacher I knew asked about my rates, I turned the question back to him: "What do you normally pay for an assembly?"

He replied, "Eighty to $120." This was a pleasant surprise because I had planned to charge only $50. In the end, I was paid $120 for my first assembly!

If you wish to begin telling in schools, call your local school districts to find out how they hire storytellers. Do you need to audition for a committee who must put you on a list of approved performers for the schools? Must you provide a résumé describing your educational background and the objectives of your storytelling workshops? Who is in charge of different departments, such as special education or library services? What is the going rate for classroom presentations, workshops, and assemblies? What types of stories are teachers most interested in? Which grade levels study which time periods and countries? What kinds of research should you conduct?

If you want to be booked by public libraries, call the director of children's services. Ask if there is an approved list of performers for summer reading club programs and how you go about getting added to the list. See if you can perform at a meeting of children's librarians so they can see who you are. Find out if there is an interest in a workshop on storytelling.

The same procedure applies if you wish to tell in any venue. Choose a group of people you wish to tell to (parents of young children, gay advocacy groups, seniors, science fiction writers, and so on). Research the market. Read publications and media for that audience; talk to people about what is important to them; if appropriate, join the organization. Send a letter of inquiry to the director of programs at the organization suggesting some of the ways your storytelling would fit into their program. Ask if you can make an appointment to find out more about their organization and its needs. If at all possible, use people you know to help you get a foot in the door.

You may have to do some free shows to demonstrate your ability. One mime I know rented an auditorium and sent out invitations to 200 potential bookers to see his program. When- ever you do a show, whether for free or for pay, send invitations to people that might hire you in the future. (Of course, make sure that it's all right for observers to come to your show. A church might not want outsiders tak- ing part in a private workshop. Parents prob- ably wouldn't like strangers wandering in to their child's backyard birthday party.)

Hitting the Bull's-Eye[2]

Once there was maggid, or a traveling teacher, who always told stories. It didn't matter if you came to him with a point of law that you wanted explained, a failing marriage that you wanted to discuss, or a grief that you wanted soothed. No matter what the problem, the maggid would tell you a story.

One day a rabbi asked him, "There are sermons you could give, books you could read from, prophets who could be quoted, lectures you could deliver. Why do you always answer every question with a story?"

Of course, the maggid replied, "Let me tell you a story.

"There was once a general who decided to take up a hobby—archery. But being a general, he pursued his hobby like he would conquer a country. It was not enough to relax and enjoy himself. No, he had to be the best archer ever born. He read every book on the subject. He hired the finest teachers from all over the world. He bought the most expensive bow and arrows. Still, he could not hit the bull's-eye every time . . . and it bothered him!

"One day he was riding in his coach to a military meeting when he saw the most amazing sight. He called for his driver to stop, jumped out of the coach, and ran into a nearby farmhouse, bursting in on a family eating dinner.

" 'Where is he?' he demanded. 'Where is the master archer who did that?' He pointed out the window at their barn. On the side of the barn were many targets drawn, and in the center of each one was a single arrow.

"The family shrugged and pushed forward a little boy about 10 years old. 'You! A mere lad is able to do what I cannot! Show me your secret.'

"The boy led the general out to the barn. He provided him with a crudely made bow and arrow and said, 'Do as I do.' He pulled back his bowstring, aimed in the general direction of the barn, closed his eyes, and let the arrow fly.

"Then he put down the bow, picked up a paint brush, dipped it into a bucket and began to paint the target around the arrow."

The maggid stopped and looked at his colleague who was listening intently. "A good rabbi is a storyteller who knows so many tales that he can fit the right one to any situation."

The End 📖

The rabbi learned from the maggid. The general learned from the child. You learned a bit about Jewish culture from this story. A true teller is willing to learn from anyone and anything and to share that knowledge through story. No matter what point you wish to make, I believe that you can hit the bull's-eye with a story.

Learning from Others

In my career as a storyteller, I've gained knowledge and skills from a wide variety of people. For example:

- A preschool teacher once told me that there are three personality types: fearful, feisty, and flexible. I began to look at my listeners as individuals who fit into those types. It helped me realize that I had to design my programs to please all types of listeners.

- A folk musician mentioned in a festival workshop that her grandma always said that the difference between a long song and a short song is that before a long song you should go to the bathroom. I filed that saying in my memory to paraphrase one day before telling a long story.

- A calligrapher explained how she sets up her fees, and I understood that I could choose to charge according to the circumstances.

- I watched a juggler begin his show by entering from the back of the audience and interacting with the children as he came to the front. I haven't done that yet, but I have begun talking and playing with audience members before my "official" show begins.

- I learned from a book on origami how to fold rabbits to hand out as party favors.

- An actress worked with me on developing my breathing.

- A dancer tried to help me move more.

- Storytellers who use sign language, such as the late Floating Eagle Feather, so enchanted me that I took an adult education class in signing. Even when I'm not using this beautiful language, I sometimes find my gestures are more expressive.

- A young man sitting next to me on an airplane told me that the Chinese believe that you cannot escape bureaucracy even after death. There are ghostly bureaucrats too.

- A young Japanese woman explained to my husband and me that Japanese ghosts have no feet.

- Teachers in a faculty lounge reminisced about the folklore of their youth, including rhymes for bouncing a ball and what to say if you see a car with only one headlight. I used their stories to ask children if contemporary folklore has changed since their parents' and grandparents' days.

- A storyteller sat down to tell during a school assembly. When I realized that some children were trying to peer around the front rows to see the teller, I made a mental note that I would always stand when telling to large groups.

- Classes and tapes have helped me expand my Spanish vocabulary, as the media projects an increase in the number of Spanish-speaking Americans in the near future.

- A professional clown explained that I was telling my stories too fast. He said that if I slowed down my physical reaction to the spoken words, I could increase the comic impact of my stories. He was right. Younger children do enjoy broad gestures and funny faces.

- A storyteller told an urban legend about a burglar who died from a dog bite. I heard a worried little boy ask her afterwards if the tale was true. She replied, "If it isn't, it ought to be." I was horrified. While that answer would be appropriate if the story was a fantasy about flying dragons, it was the wrong way to allay a small child's fears. I resolved to listen carefully when a child asks me about the truth of a tale and to respond according to what I think is really being asked. I believe that child needed to know that burglars would not be dying in his closet that night.

I think these examples demonstrate that everyone you meet and everything you read, observe, and hear is grist for your storytelling mill and can teach you to be a more effective storyteller.

You should never stop learning about the art and business of storytelling and related fields. Continue to participate in classes and workshops in storytelling, theater, voice, singing, speech, education, literature, folklore, foreign languages, pantomime, clowning, magic, juggling, visual arts, calligraphy (for signs, fliers, and thank-you notes), computers, public relations, sewing (for pretty banners and fancy costumes), psychology (to better understand your audiences and yourself), marketing, accounting, grant writing, graphic design (for fliers and brochures), creative writing, genealogy, and history. All these courses are readily available from colleges, universities, adult education programs, conferences, organizations, and individuals. Some will even be free. The library can supply you with audiotapes, videotapes, records, pamphlets, periodicals, and books on any subject. Television and the radio can be sources of educational programs. Everyone you meet is a storehouse of information. Remember, if you aren't learning at least one new thing a day, you must be dead—or deadly dull.

Learning from Peers

One of the best ways to learn is from your peers. This is not a one-way street; you also have information and advice that you can share. Learn from your colleagues by observing them at work, reading what they write, and participating in groups and workshops. Every year I join a small group of dedicated professional freelance storytellers in a retreat. I highly recommend retreats for all tellers—in fact, for all professions (librarians, ministers, teachers, social workers, and so on) who use storytelling. Retreats allow you to meet with like-minded people away from the stress of everyday life to socialize, practice stories, discuss problems, prevent creative burnout, and discover new ways of doing things.

Storytellers who have been part of our retreat in the past include Barbara Griffin, Angela Lloyd, Olga Loya, Sandra MacLees, Lee Ellen Marvin, Nancy Schimmel, and Kathleen Zundell.

Running a Retreat

My colleagues and I have certain rules for our retreats:

1. Each retreat is limited to no more than seven people. Only so much can be accomplished in two to four days. If there are too many people, less is accomplished for each.

2. Everyone shares in expenses and chores. We don't want to burden our host.

3. Everything said at the retreat is confidential. We need to be able to trust each other and to speak freely because of that trust.

The first day of a retreat is usually spent catching up on our personal and professional lives since the previous year's retreat. We then each state our goals for the retreat. These range from strengthening our friendships to voice and body work to having a daily group discussion to enjoying some quiet time to telling a story so that everyone else can critique it.

During our last night, we share our personal and professional fears. It's wonderful to be able to take off our professional, "in-control," adult masks and admit our doubts.

In between, we work on our stated goals. One of the wonderful bonuses of a retreat is getting to know, care for, and respect tellers you may not have known before. Watching tellers perform or talking casually with them at storytelling festivals isn't the same as sharing advice, successes, and fears and learning what they really want out of life.

One reason I believe that the tellers in the retreats I've attended are willing to share their secrets for success is that we all live in different areas. I realize that this can be a competitive business, so I recommend that when you set up a "working" retreat, you choose artists who work in different markets. A retreat of local artists could focus on bonding and relaxation—two very important goals—instead of the more competitive business aspects of telling.

Imitation

Maybe you decided to become a story-teller because you were inspired by a performance you heard. You probably rushed home and told the tale that touched you to a friend, possibly imitating the style and presentation of the teller who so impressed you.

Now that you intend to get up on the stage yourself, you might be tempted to use the stories and style of your favorite artist. Don't. Even if the basic stories are historical narratives, myths, or folktales, the final version of a particular teller comes about after extensive research, rewriting, and rehearsal. That includes the introduction, the segues, and any audience participation. The teller legally and morally owns his or her specific version.

Even more taboo is telling someone else's personal story.

As my colleague, storyteller Angela Lloyd, stated at our 1995 retreat, "You have a voice of your own. It takes time and trust in yourself to discover it, but if you take what seems to be the easy way of using someone else's story and style, you will be a fraud. During your performance, you will find yourself caught up in remembering how that teller did it, so you will not connect with the audience in an authentic way. You will be acting, not telling a story."

Watch and listen to tellers you admire and take note of their interactions with the audience, methods for starting and ending a show, pacing, stance, gestures, facial expressions, and voice patterns. Work on each of these aspects of telling for yourself in a new way. Slowly, as your audiences react to your tellings, you will develop a style that is unique to you.

If you want to use the stories and specific style of other tellers, first obtain their permission. If a teller won't give you permission to use their version of a story, begin to research your own version. Search for the folktale in the library, ask other tellers if they know a source for the story, or consult *The Storytellers' Sourcebook* by Margaret Read MacDonald (Detroit: Gale, 1982), which lists numerous sources of many folktales from around the world. If a story is personal or an original of that teller, you should never retell it without the author's permission. I always say that courtesy is as important as copyright. If you hear someone using another story-teller's or author's tales without acknowledging sources, talk to them afterwards. Find out if they know that they should get permission and if they have done so. If the person hasn't obtained permission and continues to use the story, please inform the author or other teller of this infringement. You would want someone to tell you if your stories were being misused. It's your responsibility as a member of the storytelling community to do the same.

Just as surely as you see performers you wish to be like, you will also watch others who will do things you hope you never do, such as the storyteller I observed sitting down where some audience members couldn't see him, and the teller who scared the child with the burglar legend that was not appropriate for the little boy's age group and then compounded the problem by making a flippant comment when the lad asked if the tale was true. Make mental notes.

Resources

Getting Started

If you want help with the business of being a freelance performer, call the Small Business Administration and ask about their services, which include free one-on-one con-sultations and low-priced workshops on subjects such as fees and marketing. Their phone number is 1-800-U-ASK-SBA. The workshops can be excellent, and hooking up with other small businesses can lead to important contacts.

Books and Articles About Storytelling

Storytelling Techniques

Tips on technique rarely go out of style. Every year new books on storytelling are published. Check your library, *Books in Print*, and the catalogs of Libraries Unlimited, August House, California Storytellers, and the National Storytelling Association for current sources.

Cassady, Marsh. *Storytelling Step by Step.* San Jose, CA: Resource Publications, 1990.
"Introductions and Conclusions" and "Delivering Your Story."

Cundiff, Ruby, and Barbara Webb. *Storytelling for You.* Yellow Springs, OH: Antioch Press, 1957.
"The Rehearsal of Your Story" and "The Presentation of Your Story."

de Vos, Gail. *Storytelling for Young Adults.* Englewood, CO: Libraries Unlimited, 1991.
"Storytelling Techniques."

de Wit, Dorothy. *Children's Faces Looking Up: Program Building for the Storyteller.* Chicago: American Library Association, 1979.
"Tips for Tellers." Also annotated lists of stories about food, animals, magical creatures, shoes and related topics, journeys, and colors. The holiday list is the only one with suggested ages.

Geisler, Harlynne. "Reminders." *The Story Bag Newsletter* (January 1990): 3.
Experienced performers Steve Sanfield and Bob Jenkins give suggestions at a story critique session to tellers on how to improve their technique.

Greene, Ellin, and George Shannon. *Storytelling: A Selected Annotated Bibliography.* New York: Garland, 1986.
Two hundred and sixty-two entries organized into eight categories: beginning, purpose and values, art and technique, special settings and needs, reading aloud, storytellers, building background, and indexes. Nine-page subject index.

Hamilton, Martha, and Mitch Weiss. *Children Tell Stories: A Teaching Guide.* Katonah, NY: Richard C. Owen, 1990.
"Helping Children Tell Their Stories."

Livo, Norma, and Sandra Reitz. *Storytelling: Process and Practice.* Littleton, CO: Libraries Unlimited, 1986.
"Preparing, Developing and Delivering Stories."

MacDonald, Margaret Read. *The Storyteller's Start-Up Book: Finding, Learning, Performing and Using Folktales.* Little Rock, AR: August House, 1993.
"Performing the Story."

Maguire, Jack. *Creative Storytelling: Choosing, Inventing, and Sharing Tales for Children.* New York: McGraw-Hill, 1985.
"Telling Stories."

Pellowski, Anne. *The World of Storytelling.* Bronx, NY: H. W. Wilson, 1990.
"The Format and Style of Storytelling [in Europe, Asia, and Africa]."

Ross, Ramon. *Storyteller.* Columbus, OH: Charles E. Merrill, 1972.
"Sharing the Story."

Sawyer, Ruth. *The Way of the Storyteller.* New York: Viking, 1962.
"A Technique to Abolish Technique."

Schimmel, Nancy. *Just Enough to Make a Story: A Sourcebook for Storytelling.* Berkeley, CA: Sisters' Choice Books & Recordings, 1992.
"Telling a Story." Available from 1639 Channing Way, Berkeley, CA 94703, 510-843-0533.

Shedlock, Marie. *The Art of the Story-teller.* New York: Dover, 1951.
"The Artifices of Story-telling" and "How to Obtain and Maintain the Effect of the Story."

Thompson, Richard. "Have Your Wolf to Tea." *The Story Bag Newsletter* (July 1988): 3–4.

The importance of knowing the characters in your stories.

Sources

MacDonald, Margaret Read. *The Storytellers' Sourcebook: A Subject, Title, and Motif Index to Folklore Collections for Children.* Detroit: Gale, 1982.

Periodicals

Subscription rates can change. Write for current rates before sending a check.

Laugh Makers: The Variety Arts Magazine for Kidshow and Family Audience Entertainers
P.O. Box 160
Syracuse, NY 13215
Ph: 315-492-4523
Six issues/year. 1995 subscription rate was $24 ($30 outside the United States).
The best magazine for both business and performance information on clowning, magic, puppetry, balloons, and many other variety arts.

The Story Bag: A National Storytelling Newsletter
5361 Javier Street
San Diego CA 92117-3215
Ph: 619-569-9399
Call for fax number and current email address.
Six issues/year. Subscription rate is $20 ($25 outside North America). The subscription rate for two years is $38. Photocopies of back issues may be purchased for $5 each. (California residents please add sales tax to photocopy cost.)
Every issue has a column on how to be a professional freelance storyteller; a column called "Tips on Technique"; a "Storytelling Activities in the Classroom" section; the full text of a story; a "Reader Asks" column; reviews of books and tapes;

and a two-page listing of storytelling events in the United States, Canada, and the rest of the world.

Storyline
1 Rochdale Way
Berkeley, CA 94708
Four issues/year. 1995 subscription rate was $15.
Includes "Dear Kate," an advice column in which editor Kate Frankel answers questions sent in by readers. Every issue also includes the most complete listing of events in northern California.

Storytelling Magazine
National Storytelling Association
P.O. Box 309
Jonesborough, TN 37659
Ph: 615-753-2171
Toll free: 800-525-4514
Six issues/year. 1995 subscription rates was $40 ($50 in Canada).
Includes how-to articles on telling and teaching using storytelling.

Further Reading

Erickson, Judith. *Directory of Youth Organizations: 1994–1995: A Guide to 500 Clubs, Groups, Troops, Teams, Societies, Lodges and More for Young People.* Minneapolis, MN: Free Spirit, 1994.

This listing of national nonprofit associations for young people 18 and under will lead you to groups that might wish to hire a storyteller on the local, regional, or national level. If you want to market yourself to camps, see the *1994–95 Guide to Accredited Camps*, which lists 2,100 summer camps (800-428-CAMP), and the Western Association of Independent Camps free directory of 50 camps (800-758-7519).

Finley, Stewart. "Defining the Storytelling Genre." *The Story Bag Newsletter* (November 1990): 1–3.

Notes

1. National Council of Teachers of English, "Teaching Storytelling: A Position Statement from the Committee on Storytelling" (Urbana, IL: National Council of Teachers of English, n.d.).

2. "Hitting the Bull's-Eye" was told by Rabbi Jacob Kranz, the Maggid of Dubno [Poland] (1741–1804), who was known as the Jewish Aesop because he developed the parable as a teaching tale. A *rabbi* is a Jewish preacher. A *maggid* is a traveling teacher who explains the Torah through stories and sermons. The tale of the bull's-eye was a well-known joke, but the Maggid used it to explain how he used stories to teach. I changed the gun in the original story to a bow and arrow because I don't like guns. Other versions of the story include: Peninnah Schram, ed., "The Bull's Eye," in *Jewish Stories One Generation Tells Another* (Northvale, NJ: Jason Aronson, 1987), 2–5; and Nathan Ausubel, ed., "Hitting the Bull's Eye," in *A Treasury of Jewish Folklore: Stories, Traditions, Legends, Humor, Wisdom and Folk Songs of the Jewish People* (New York: Crown, 1948), 4.

Chapter 2

Performing

Though this book will not cover the basics of learning and telling a story (a subject covered beautifully by many other books), it is important to know how to perform in a professional manner.

Organizing Your Shows into Themes

You will find it easier to market your performances if you have shows based on specific themes. Consider your target audience as well as your repertoire when designing a show's theme. For example, if you are selling to churches, you might consider focusing on "Miracles and Marvels"—stories of holy or spiritual people and fictional or true events that show God's hand. If your target audience is a retirement home, a theme such as "Those Were the Good Old Days" or "Older *and* Better" might sell. If you are telling to women's groups, you can either create a feminist-oriented show such as "Yes, Women Can" or one that focuses on other women's issues, such as "For Better or Worse: Tales of Marriage and Family."

Children always enjoy spooky stories (less spooky for the younger ones), so you could name your show "Boo! Stories to Scare Your Socks Off." Kids also like shows with animal themes such as "Raining Cats and Dogs: Tales About Pets" or "Lions and Tigers and Bears: Oh, My!"

Titles

No matter what theme you select, an intriguing title will help sell the show to both bookers and audiences. The title should be clear enough to give potential listeners some idea of what to expect. Check with your booker about how much space your show will be given in the publicity. I once gave a workshop titled "Got a Minute? Short, Short Folktales" for a folk festival. However, only the main part of the title "Got a Minute?" was printed in the program, and no one could figure out what my workshop would be about.

Collecting Stories

Once you've chosen a theme (or had one chosen for you by the booker or the season), you need to research appropriate stories. Head to your local library. Check the card catalog or computer under all subject headings related to your theme. Ask the librarian to show you reference books that might list stories by subject, such as *The Storyteller's Sourcebook: A Subject, Title, and Motif Index to Folklore Collections for Children* by Margaret Read MacDonald. Don't look only at folktales. Check out short-story collections and nonfiction books. For instance, you might include a true story about someone's pet in a "Raining Cats and Dogs" show.

Look at the dictionaries of quotations and *Brewer's Dictionary of Phrase and Fable* for sayings that you could use to begin your program or to tie one story to another. When I was performing my show "Toads and Diamonds: Jewels in Fairy Tales," I used several short quotations, such as "Diamond cuts diamond" and "Do not cast pearls before swine."

Check nonfiction books for interesting facts that you can use between stories. When I was researching "Monsters, Monsters, Monsters," I found out that other cultures had legends not only about werewolves, but also about werebears and weretigers. For the program "For Better or Worse," about marriage, you might check the latest edition of the *Guinness Book of World Records* for the lengths of the shortest and the longest marriages ever. Check joke and riddle books for amusing things to say about your subject. Or if you like, look in songbooks for something to sing on the subject.

Once you've left the library, don't forget to use human resources, including events from your own or others' lives. Just be sure to get your aunt Matilda's permission before you share her haunted house experience with the public.

I generally find more stories and "stretchers" (those interesting facts, jokes, songs, etc.) than I can use in a single show, so I select the ones most suitable for my intended audience. A certain tale may be great for kids, but adults might consider the same story too childish. Adults might laugh at a pun that is too sophisticated for a kindergarten audience.

Once I've decided on my tales and stretchers, it's time to buckle down, create my show, and rehearse it until it's ready to take on the road. I work with the organization of the show, trying to decide which arrangement would work best. Do I want to begin with a ridiculous pun and a couple of unusual facts? If so, the first story should probably be amusing. Then I might want to change the tone with a longer, more thoughtful story. Do I want to end on a laugh? As I work with the show, some items just won't fit, and I put them aside, possibly to be used in a different show.

It's a Good Day to Tell Stories: Holiday Themes

Any special day or recognition period, from Halloween to National Pig Week, can be celebrated with appropriate tales. These special events include National Women's History Month (March), Children's Book Week (November), National Library Week (April), Earth Day (April 22), Native American Day (May 14), Mexican Independence Day (September 15), International Day of Peace (September 17), Rudyard Kipling's birthday (December 30), Jacob Grimm's birthday (January 4), and . . . well, you get the idea. Every day is International Story Day. An excellent way to keep track of these important dates is to get the "Storyteller's Calendar" or the "Myth and Magic" calendar. The addresses to order these calendars are listed in the "Resources" section at the end of this chapter.

Two books that suggest shows with particular themes are Dorothy de Wit's *Children's Faces Looking Up: Program Building for the Storyteller* and Caroline Bauer's *New Handbook for Storytellers.*

Building a Repertoire

You must build a repertoire before you can advertise yourself. If you only know three stories, you'll likely be asked to tell for some event at which these tales won't work.

How many stories should you know before becoming a freelance performer? There's no set number, but I recommend that you develop an extensive collection as part of paying your dues before expecting others to pay you. If you ask for payment but give an amateurish performance, with inappropriate stories, you will give not only yourself but all other storytellers a bad name.

Building an Audience

Choose which audiences you plan to focus on: preschool, elementary, secondary, adult, retirement homes, churches, and so on. Do several free shows to get experience telling in front of an audience. Ask the people who book you for the free shows to "pay" you by writing letters that tell what you did right and suggest improvements. These written comments can later be used in your brochures, press releases, and résumés.

I still request written feedback in my performance contract. I select comments targeted to potential bookers for my résumés. For instance, if a church wants to know what others have said about my religious shows and workshops, I can create a résumé that lists churches I have worked for, specific spiritual programs that I have created, favorable remarks from religious bookers, and quotations from articles.

Performing free shows will help you work the kinks out of your act and give you a better sense of where you feel comfortable telling. You may decide that little kids are brats, and you prefer performing for seniors. Or you may realize that you're actually a third-grader at heart, and adults just won't laugh at your silly puns. Slowly the types of audiences you are comfortable with will grow.

I still do free shows at one venue: a local fourth-grade teacher is always happy to let me practice my new stories on her students.

Set the Stage and Begin the Show

Voice

This is the most important tool of any teller. In chapter 13 I cover how to handle some typical voice problems, such as not speaking loudly enough to be heard by all of your listeners.

I remember being told many years ago to leave room in my pacing to speed up at exciting parts and slow down to describe something or to create a spooky atmosphere. If you're a motor-mouth, you won't be able to speed up during a chase scene without leaving your listeners in the dust.

So many people are afraid of silence. They fill the spaces between words with such phrases as, "I mean," "You know," "Umm," and so on. Silence is a powerful tool. It gives the audience time to think about what you just said and to react to it. The more confident comedians tell a joke, and then stop and wait for the laughter as their audience "gets it."

You also need silence for thinking and reacting to your own story as you tell it. When you are repeating dialogue in a story you are telling, be careful to pause between each character's speech so that you can think for a moment and *react* to what the last character said as you speak the lines of the character who is replying. For instance, Little Red Riding Hood's dialogue with the wolf in Grandma's clothing shouldn't be rote, "What big eyes you have, Grandma"; "The better to see you with," and so on. Imagine that you are the wolf, worrying that Little Red's suspicions might make her run out of the cottage before you can pounce on that juicy morsel. How do you explain your wolf-sized eyes? All this internal dialogue goes on in a second or to, but if you don't pause and think, your wolf will be unreal and the conversation flat. Pauses also serve as invisible quotation marks so that the listeners realize that one character has stopped talking and another character has started.

Movement

Nervousness is often communicated through hands. They tremble, adjust clothes, play with hair, drop in and out of pockets, wring each other, straighten nearby objects, and otherwise distract the audience from attending to your words. If you find nervous hands a problem, try sitting as you tell and letting your hands rest quietly in your lap.

I was critiquing ninth-grade students to whom I had taught storytelling. I noticed that one girl's fear showed through her use of limited gestures. She kept her elbows close to her sides and only moved her forearms. She was standing in front of her peers who were seated in the usual classroom desks. At one point in her story the student moved her right arm to signify a sprawled dead body. As I explained to her in my critique, the students at the back of the classroom could not see that gesture because it was made at waist length. I told her that if she was standing higher than her audience, everyone would be able to see her arm and hand motions. If the teller is on a stage or if the audience is seated on the floor while the teller sits on a chair or stands, all her gestures would be seen be everyone.

As a general rule, gestures should be made from the shoulder rather than from the elbow. Obviously, an experienced performer knows when to break this rule, but beginners are often nervous. Wishing to protect themselves from the audience, they often keep their arms close to their bodies, sometimes even clasping their hands in front of them.

Try saying, "They went that-away," pointing to the right while keeping your right elbow pinned to your waist. Observe yourself in the mirror as you do this. You will see how awkward the gesture looks. Now say, "They went that-away," and point to the right in a grand sweeping gesture that involves your whole arm. Notice in the mirror how much more dramatic this movement looks than the previous one. Your audience will have no trouble seeing which way you are pointing— even those listeners seated in the back row.

There will be times when a movement from the shoulder rather than from the elbow will not be the correct choice. For instance, if you were portraying a timid mouse telling a ferocious lion, "They went that-away," it would be appropriate to show the mouse's fear through the smaller gesture.

If you wish to add a wonderful ingredient to flavor your telling, learn sign language. I have often had students with family members who are hearing impaired speak to me after a show. They are so proud of knowing the signs I used. It helps validate the beauty and importance of this wonderful language for all students, not just those with hearing impairments. Also, it will give you something to do with those nervous hands!

If you are not stuck behind a microphone on a stand, you can add more than just gesture to flavor your performance. Olga Loya dances onto the stage to start one of her stories about going to high school parties. Taking dance, gymnastics, and theater classes will teach you more about how to use your body to portray characters and mood. Always be aware of whether your choice of movement (such as falling to the ground) truly adds to the story or whether it makes it difficult for audience members to see you. There is a school of storytelling that was begun in the New York Public Library in the 1940s that forbids gestures and movement. I could never have trained in that school as I naturally use my hands as I talk, but I do agree that often "less is more."

Videotape your performance of the same tale in different venues. Also have a fellow teller observe you in concert and focus on your gestures and movement. (Be sure to choose someone whose philosophy of performance agrees with your own.) Through your own observation of the videotapes and your colleague's suggestions, refine your gestures and movement.

Music

Music can be a wonderful addition to your program. You can start and end your show with music. You can sing or play an instrument as a transition between tales. The audience can sing along or listen appreciatively.

An instrument such as the drums or flute can add atmosphere to your telling as it is played softly underneath the spoken words or during a dramatic pause in the story. It can be played by you or a partner.

Songs are sometimes an integral part of stories. (I've included a short bibliography of books, which includes the musical notations for the songs in their stories, at the end of this chapter.) You can teach the audience the words so they can sing along. Young children especially enjoy doing this. If you prefer not to sing, you can recite or chant the song or merely describe what happens in the lyrics.

Props

Caroline Feller Bauer recommends that you have a storytelling symbol, such as a banner with Anansi the Spider or a Peter Rabbit doll. This symbol will soon become identified with you.

Props can be used to intrigue your audiences, educate them, or prepare them to listen. You can use special objects to identify yourself as a storyteller. You can use certain objects, such as a hat, vine, or staff with objects dangling from it, to represent different stories. In such cases, allow a child from your audience to choose which story you will tell by pointing to one of the objects. When I was a librarian, I wore an apron with five different-colored pockets made for me by a fellow storyteller. I would let a child reach into a pocket and remove the toy or story card in that pocket. Then I would tell the tale represented. If I wanted to choose the order of the stories, I would direct the child to choose from a certain pocket.

Use an interesting or unique box to represent the story of how Anansi the Spider tricked the Sun God into giving him the box that held all the stories in the world. Have a boy or girl open the box to release the tale you are about to share. At the end of your show, have another child pretend to catch the story, return it to the box, and close the lid.

Other tellers use props in special ways. Chief Don Lelooska begins his concerts by loudly beating a drum—a very dramatic way to capture the listeners' attention. Many folktales from different cultures mention drums.

The Seneca and Iroquois tribes say that all the world's stories were told to a boy by a stone he discovered. Use a beautiful stone as a prop when telling this tale.

Another way to "set the stage," and prepare your audience, is to bring an artifact from the culture or time of your story for them to see or touch before you begin. Jim Silverman, California historian and storyteller and owner of the Kids' History Company, wishes he could present students with a "scratch and sniff" history so they could physically experience life as it was back then. Instead he brings in objects that they can feel, smell, and use before he tells them tales about the past.

The "Resources" section at the end of this chapter lists companies from which you can obtain cultural artifacts.

Stages and Seats

Author and storyteller Pleasant DeSpain stands on a small Persian rug when he performs. Children call it his magic carpet. Josephine Pedersen of Port Angeles, Washington, uses a colorful, washable quilt. She spreads it out for the children to sit on as they enjoy her stories.

Whenever possible, I have my listeners sit on the floor. Chairs, tables, and desks are physical and mental barriers that often keep individual listeners from feeling that they are part of the group. I am part of their group too, so I sit or stand as close to my audience as possible. Physical distance destroys intimacy. Do not stand behind a table, podium, or desk or on a stage to tell stories unless absolutely necessary. Make sure you can see everyone in your audience. If you can't see everyone, you can't be seen by everyone. Rearrange the seating if possible or move around during the show so everyone can observe the performance.

Beginnings and Endings to Shows

I usually begin my shows informally: welcoming the classes as they file into the room, chatting with the students, asking riddles, doing string figures, showing off my storyteller doll necklace, or playing games and doing finger plays with the younger students. I try to be approachable, acting as hostess to the story world the audience will soon be entering. Listeners often decide whether you're any good before you've even started telling. Older children and adolescents especially need to be wooed, as they are afraid to seem "babyish."

After each show I answer questions, listen to the students' own stories, repeat funny voices they liked, and accept compliments. As any good story hostess would, I thank them for coming and for being such great listeners. The last person I thank is the principal. If the principal is busy, I leave a message with the secretary. If possible, I compliment the school in some way.

I always try to allow time to talk to my adult audiences as well. My husband knows not to expect me for up to an hour after a show or workshop; some people can be long-winded. However, interaction after the show is important to your business. Compliment the booker on how clear their directions to the show were or something about their person, such as a pretty blouse or a wonderfully deep voice. Sympathize with them over their difficulties. Take notes about the people you talk with so you can ask about their children by name the next time you see them. Refer to your notes before a repeat visit.

Beginnings and Endings to Stories

Michael Parent says that a good story has a hook, line, and sinker. Many of my stories have hooks that begin before the first line of the story. They are the introductions. An example is: "You might have guessed because of my red hair and silver tongue that I have a wee bit of the Irish in me. My grandfather's name was Ralph McLaughlin, and his grandfather was from the Emerald Isle. You may also know that the Irish love ghost stories. I'd like to share one with you now."

One thing I never say before a story is that I'm going to tell a funny or a scary one. It sets up unreal expectations and resistance. If you announce that you're going to tell a funny story, some children will make a point of not laughing or of laughing in a rude, artificial way. A big part of humor is surprise, so let your audience discover the jokes as you proceed with the story.

Ghost stories are just not as frightening in a well-lighted room as when you are huddling together at night in a dark room at a slumber party, so some kids may be disappointed by daylight ghost stories. In spite of this, I never turn off the lights, even when the children beg me, because the bolder children will misbehave in the dark, and the more timid children will become too frightened. I may dim the lights a bit, though.

Some stories have perfect endings that wrap the story up so that no one doubts that it's over. Other stories seem to dangle. It's bound to happen sometime: you say the last line of the tale and wait for the audience's response. They just gaze at you expectantly. Oops! They don't realize the story is over. To avoid this, you can conclude some stories with formula sayings such as "And that was the story of . . ." Or you can finish with, "And they lived . . ." Pause, and the children will call out with you, " . . . happily ever after."

You might also choose to end with a simple poem such as:

Snip, snap, snout;
My tale's told out.

You can find poems to end tales in *The World of Storytelling* by Anne Pelowski and *Italian Folktales* by Italo Calvino.

Audience Participation

I once observed a storyteller using a participatory story. He taught his family audience a short song that was repeated throughout the story. Everyone knew what they were supposed to do, but not when. The teller gave no warning about when to sing the song, so that by the time people realized they were supposed to be singing along, the song would be half finished. As the story went on, fewer and fewer audience members were singing. It's hard to get adults to sing in public anyway, and they felt foolish not knowing exactly when to participate. The children were looking to their parents as role models and probably sensing their embarrassment and reluctance.

Especially when I'm working with younger children, I want them to feel successful, so I give them easily understood cues about when to participate. We practice the participation roles before launching the story. When I come to the places in the story where the audience gets involved, I start the first gesture while looking into the eyes of the children, pause for just a second to see that they are ready to begin their participation, and *then* continue.

Even if I am only asking the children to repeat words, I use a visual cue. For example, in my version of the fairy tale, "Lazy Jack," I look surprised and put my hand on my cheek every time Jack says, "Oh! Next time I'll know what to do." This prepares the children to say the words with me.

While I would never tell older students that I expect them to repeat words with me, I do something kind of sneaky in some of my stories. I use what I call "compelling language." By this I mean phrases or sentences that are repeated throughout a story. I say the words slowly and in an amusing way. The kids hear the way I say the words and find themselves saying it along with me, partly to mock me, and partly to test their ability to say the words in the same tone of voice. An example of a story with compelling language is "You'll Be Sorry," my version of a story sometimes called "The Yellow Ribbon." When I say the repeated phrase, "but . . . you'll be sorry," I pause after the word *but*, look mischievous, and then say "you'll be sor-ree!" with my voice rising on the end of the last word. By the time I get to the last sentence, I can pause and let the audience say "sor-ree" for me. Here's the full text of the story:

You'll Be Sorry: A Texas Tale

There was this little boy and this little girl who lived next door to each other. Every day they would walk to school together. Now, there was one thing that was weird about that little girl: she always wore a red bandanna tied around her neck. It didn't matter if she had on an orange blouse or a pink T-shirt. She always wore that ugly red bandanna.

That little boy began to wonder about it. One day he says to her, "Why do you always wear that red bandanna?"

She says, "I could take it off, but . . . you'll be sorry!"

He decided that it wasn't that important.

They kept walking to school together through grade school and junior high. When they got to high school, they began dating each other. He asked her to the senior prom, and she agreed to go.

That night he came to pick her up in his daddy's car. She had on a real pretty pink dress—but she was still wearing that red bandanna, just like every day. He says to her, he says, "Can't you take it off for the dance? I mean, think how it'll look in the pictures!"

She says, "I could, but . . . you'll be sorry!"

He decided that it wasn't going to look that bad.

They graduated, went to college, got jobs . . . and kept falling deeper and deeper in love. One day he asked her if she'd marry him, and she said, "Yes."

So there he was, all nervous and excited in his best suit, standing at the altar. The doors at the back of the church opened, and in she came on her daddy's arm, just a vision of loveliness in a long white dress . . . and then he saw it, underneath the veil: that ugly red bandanna!

Oh, he was so embarrassed! When she stood next to him, he whispered to her, "Couldn't you take it off for the wedding?"

She whispered back, "Well, I could have, but . . . you'll be sorry!" He loved her so much that that day he took two vows. He took the wedding vows, and he swore to himself that he'd never again ask her about that red bandanna. He kept that promise.

They had children and then grandchildren. Soon they were getting on in years, and her time had come.

He was there by her hospital bed, just feeling so bad. She says to him, "You've been a good husband all these years, and you never again asked me about my red bandanna. Well, I'll tell you what. If you want to take it off when I'm dead, you can, but . . . you'll be sorry!" Then she was gone.

He cried a bit, but he couldn't help looking at that bandanna. He really had wondered all those years, and she'd said it was okay.

He reached behind her neck and gently untied the knot . . . and her head rolled off the bed and bounced on the floor.

And he was sorry!

The End 📖

Costumes

Sometimes when people call, especially around Halloween, they ask what type of costume I wear. I once saw a teller wearing a witch's outfit with her face painted green narrate a story about two children and their experiences with a witch. I found it jarring to watch the witch speak the children's dialogue. Nancy Duncan, a storyteller and actress in Nebraska, sometimes dressed as Baba Yaga, the famous witch of Russian fairy tales. Unfortunately, some people assumed that if she dressed as a witch, she must be a witch. This evil rumor spread and caused her great difficulties.

I usually tell my potential bookers that I prefer not to dress as one character from a story because as a storyteller I am *all* the characters as well as the narrator. This philosophy cost me a booking at a shopping mall where they wanted me to dress as Mrs. Santa Claus or a fairy princess. Though I would have liked the money, I would have felt silly standing next to Santa's house trying to tell stories to passersby.

Instead I prefer to create an atmosphere with my choice of clothes. I might wear a black dress, owl necklace, and skeleton earrings to my spooky tales performances. A dress from Guatemala or India puts me in the mood for folk tales from around the world. When I wear my Pueblo storyteller doll necklace and earrings, I point them out and tell the listeners that no one can tell a story as well as someone who loves you and holds you in his or her lap. I enjoy wearing gold shoes when I stand in front of a group of children seated on the floor; they always notice. My socks or hose often have sparkles on them. If I am performing at a Renaissance fair, I wear clothing of the time. In December I wear festive red and green or blue and silver with earrings that are symbols of either Christmas or Hanukkah.

On two occasions bookers have talked me into a more costumed look. One mother wanted me to wear a ball gown while telling the story of "Cinderella" at her daughter's party. At another party I agreed to wear a witch's hat. But in both cases, I felt uncomfortable and unconvincing.

Whatever I wear is in good repair and different from ordinary street clothes, so that without my saying a word, people know that I am the storyteller. I mention my clothes being in good repair because I once worked as a duo with a man whose T-shirt was torn, and I heard people commenting unfavorably about this after the show. Though his stories were energetic and fun, I knew that he wouldn't be asked back. Many male tellers wear a hat, suspenders, and a colorful tie.

Try the clothes out before wearing them for a show. I always pick tops that won't show perspiration stains. I learned the hard way that I must practice my gestures dressed in my performance clothing in front of a mirror. One dress I wore to a show was so loose that the neckline kept shifting as I waved my arms. A blouse that looked beautiful when my arms were down had such big armholes that everyone could see my slip when I raised my arms to signify the bear in my story.

If you enjoy dressing up, feel comfortable telling in costume, and if you are telling stories that won't "clash" with the costume, go right ahead. If you are telling stories for a show that is all from one character's viewpoint, it may be appropriate to dress as that person. If you have decided to take on a persona, such as a sea captain who tells ocean narratives and sings chanteys, or you are sharing stories only from your own ethnic background and have garb of that tradition, a costume may be suitable.

Whenever you appear in your storyteller attire, you will be noticed. So be careful not to do anything that would seem improper. A "Mother Goose" who smoked in public, for example, would be a no-no.

Even when you are not in costume, you can identify yourself as the storyteller by wearing a T-shirt with a storyteller slogan. Design your own shirt, or order from one of the companies listed in the "Resources" section.

Resources

Props

Ethnic Arts and Facts
P.O. Box 20550
Oakland, CA 94620
Ph: 510-465-0451

Kids' History Company
P.O. Box 1521
Sonoma, CA 95476
Ph: 707-996-0121
Toll free: 800-996-0121
Fax: 707-938-8718
    A mail-order catalog of books and tapes that emphasizes California and American history from the viewpoint of children and of many cultures.

T-Shirts

California Storytellers
6695 Westside Road
Healdsburg, CA 95448
Ph: 707-433-8728

Elicia Designs
5730 West Abraham Lane
Glendale, AZ 85308
Ph: 602-561-1504
    Sweatshirts and tote bags also available.

Gudrun Godare
Tucson Area Reading Council
2016 East 9th Street
Tucson, AZ 85719
Ph: 520-882-9707
    Sweatshirts and note cards also available.

Nevy's California Traditional Music Society
    Country Store
20029 Burin Avenue
Torrance, CA 90503

Storylines
P.O. Box 7416
Saint Paul, MN 55107
Ph: 612-643-4321

Anansi Folktales

Aardema, Verna. *The Sky-God Stories.* New York: Coward-McCann, 1960.

Courlander, Harold, and Albert Kofi Prempeh. *The Hat-Shaking Dance, and Other Tales from the Gold Coast.* New York: Harcourt, Brace, 1957.

Haley, Gail E. *A Story, A Story: An African Tale.* New York: Atheneum, 1970.

Haviland, Virginia. *The Fairy Tale Treasury.* New York: Coward, McCann, & Geoghegan, 1972.

Sherlock, Philip M. *Anansi the Spider Man: Jamaican Folk Tales.* New York: Crowell, 1954.

————. *West Indian Folk-Tales.* New York: Walck, 1966.

Drum Folktales

There are many folktales that mention drums. These are just three sources:

Aardema, Verna. *The Riddle of the Drum: A Tale from Tizapan.* New York: Four Winds, 1979.

Burton, William. *The Magic Drum: Tales from Central Africa.* New York: Criterion, 1961.

Tooze, Ruth. *Three Tales of Monkey; Ancient Folk Tales from the Far East.* San Jose, CA: Day, 1968.

Iroquois and Seneca Stone Stories

Bruchac, Joseph. *Turkey Brother and Other Tales: Iroquois Folk Stories.* Trumansburg, NY: Crossing Press, 1975.

Cunningham, Caroline. *The Talking Stone.* New York: Knopf, 1939.

de Wit, Dorothy. *The Talking Stone: An Anthology of Native American Tales and Legends.* New York: Greenwillow, 1979.

Sanfield, Steve. *Singing Up the Mountains: Native American Tales Told by Steve Sanfield.* 1981. Audiocassette. Order from Nita, Inc., 604 Hirth Road, Columbia, MO 65201.

Storytelling Calendars

Myth and Magic Calendar
Llewellyn Publications
P.O. Box 64383
St. Paul, MN 55164-0383
Ph: 612-291-1970
Toll free: 800-843-6666
> Monthly commentaries on famous characters of mythology by storyteller Laura Simms and listings of special days, such as the birthday of the Sumerian Queen of Heaven, the Italian feast of Befana, and the Japanese Seven Herbs Festival.

Storyteller's Calendar
Stotter Press
P.O. Box 726
Stinson Beach, CA 94970
Ph: 415-435-3568
> This beautifully illustrated calendar contains complete stories from many cultures and quotations about storytelling. Each month lists famous people's birthdays, dates of storytelling festivals, and important holidays and events such as International Museum Day and Limerick Day.

Further Reading

Anderson, William, and Patrick Groff. *A New Look at Children's Literature.* Hartford, CT: Wadsworth, 1972.
> See pages 240–52 for an annotated list of books on mythology, folklore, and related forms, with suggested ages noted.

Baltuck, Naomi. *Crazy Gibberish and Other Story Hour Stretches (from a Storyteller's Bag of Tricks).* Hamden, CT: Linnet Books, 1993.
> Chants, games, songs, and stories. An audiocassette is also available.

Barton, Bob. *Tell Me Another*. Markham, ON: Pembroke, 1986.

Bauer, Caroline. *New Handbook for Storytellers*. Chicago: American Library Association, 1993.
Annotated bibliographies on various subjects and holidays. Programs for preschool and primary, intermediate, and young adult/adult groups.

Butler, Francelia. *Sharing Literature with Children: A Thematic Anthology*. New York: David McKay, 1977.
Folk rhymes, plays, tales, myths, selections from novels, and suggested reading lists organized around the themes such as toys and games, masks and shadows, gender roles, fools, and circles.

Calvino, Italo. *Italian Folktales*. New York: Harcourt Brace Jovanovich, 1980.

Clarkson, Atelia, and Gilbert Cross. *World Folktales: A Scribner Resource Collection*. New York: Charles Scribner's Sons, 1980.
An anthology organized by such subjects such as trickster tales, morality tales, and stories of witches and devils.

de Wit, Dorothy. *Children's Faces Looking Up: Program Building for the Storyteller*. Chicago: American Library Association, 1979.
Annotated lists of stories about food, animals, magical creatures, shoes and related topics, journeys, and colors. The holiday list is the only one with suggested ages.

Evans, Ivor H. *Brewer's Dictionary of Phrase and Fable*. New York: Harper & Row, 1981.

Geisler, Harlynne. "Got a Minute? Tell a Story: Short, Short Tales." *Story Bag Newsletter* (February/March 1989): 3–4.

Humphries, Tom, Carol Padden, and Terrence J. O'Rourke. *A Basic Course in American Sign Language*. Silver Spring, MD: T.J. Publishers, 1980.

Kleefeld, Jim. *The Volunteer Book: How to Select, Use and Make the Most of Your Audience Volunteers*. 33510 Jennie Road, Avon, OH 44011-2042; 216-937-5488.
How to prepare, select, use, reward, and dismiss a volunteer from the audience.

Livo, Norma. *Joining In: An Anthology of Audience Participation Stories and How to Tell Them*. Cambridge, MA: Yellow Moon Press, 1988.

MacDonald, Margaret Read. *The Storyteller's Sourcebook: A Subject, Title, and Motif Index to Folklore Collections for Children*. Detroit: Gale, 1982.
Also has ethnic and geographic indexes, including American Indian tribes. New edition expected soon.

———. *Twenty Tellable Tales: Audience Participation Folktales for the Beginning Storyteller*. Bronx, NY: H. W. Wilson, 1986.

Pellowski, Anne. *The World of Storytelling*. Bronx, NY: H. W. Wilson, 1990.

Riekehof, Lottie. *The Joy of Signing: The New Illustrated Guide for Mastering Sign Language and the Manual Alphabet*. Springfield, MO: Gospel, 1978.

Schimmel, Nancy. *Just Enough to Make a Story: A Sourcebook for Storytelling*. Berkeley, CA: Sisters' Choice Books & Recordings, 1992.
Includes an "Active Heroines in Folktales for Children" list and a "Sisters' Choices" list. Provides suggested ages, including tales for adults.

Tashjian, Virginia. *Juba This and Juba That*. New York: Little, Brown, 1969.
Tashjian's books include wonderful story stretchers.

———. *With a Deep Sea Smile*. New York: Little Brown, 1974.

Books That Include Musical Notations for Songs in the Stories

Robinson, Adjai. *Singing Tales of Africa*. New York: Scribner's, 1974.

Serwadda, W. Moses. *Songs and Stories from Uganda*. New York: Crowell, 1974.

Tracey, Hugh. *The Lion on the Path: And Other African Stories*. New York: Praeger, 1967.

Wolkstein, Diane. *The Magic Orange Tree: And Other Haitian Folktales*. New York: Knopf, 1978.

Chapter 3

Being Professional

Prepare Yourself for a Show or Workshop

Do I even need to mention rehearsals? Of course, before you give a workshop or performance you will have planned the event carefully, decided on the order of stories and stretchers, and practiced until you feel confident.

If the place or group you are performing for is new to you, see if you can look over the space in advance. When I was to perform in a large stadium, I went there weeks in advance, stood on my mark, and looked at the bleachers and thought about how I would sweep my gaze over such a large crowd. If you've never performed for preschoolers, ask a friend with young children if you might practice on them.

If you can't check out the space and audience before the day of the event, get there early and look over the situation and talk to a listener or two before going on. Warm up before a performance by doing some voice and breathing exercises. Warm up your body as well with some light physical activity. Eat only lightly before a performance so you won't feel stuffed. Don't drink caffeinated or carbonated beverages if they make you jittery or upset your stomach.

Prepare yourself mentally by visualizing a crowd of rapt listeners who will give you a standing ovation. Think over any parts of your presentation that might give you trouble and decide exactly what your first words are going to be.

Finally, check one last time to make sure your fly is zipped, your slip is not showing, your teeth are free of lipstick and food particles, your hair is combed, and your tie is straight. Ready? Set. Go.

When Does Your Performance Begin?

The instant you can be seen by any member of your audience, you should have a smile on your face and a pleasant lilt to your voice. That means you are "on" while you are still in the parking lot, if there is anyone who can observe you.

As you wait for your audience to assemble, discuss the value of storytelling with the principal, PTA president, pastor, rabbi, or other booker. It never hurts to keep selling them on storytelling's importance, and it can lead to repeat bookings. If you wish to be introduced, give your emcee a brief introduction to read.

I never consider myself "off" until I am out of sight of all audience members. I'm still smiling and waving as I drive away.

Prepare Your Bookers for a Show or Workshop

Try to Eliminate Distractions

Tell your booker that you want the audience to have the best possible experience, and that they will enjoy themselves more if they are physically comfortable with no visual or auditory distractions. If you express your requests as benefiting the audience, you won't be perceived as difficult or a prima donna.

If you're going to be performing at an event where other stages and activities will be going on, try to be placed in an area where there won't be direct competition for your listeners' attention. If there are bands scheduled, try to get performance times when your single voice won't be drowned out by their many instruments.

I remember performing at a street fair in Lemon Grove, California. The rock band's stage was directly across the street from me, and perhaps because everyone was gathered around me to listen, the band cranked their volume way up. My listeners just came in closer, and everything was going swimmingly until the bubble maker set up right next to my stage and began blowing bubbles. Then I lost them in droves. It's hard to compete with visual activities.

Don't forget to ask that any repair or maintenance work such as mowing not be done near your performance location. It's a good idea to remind the booker of this when you actually arrive. If possible, ask the custodian yourself to refrain from noisy activity within listening distance of your performance. If such disruptions occur, you will have to decide whether to stop in the middle of a story or to wait until that story's end to ask for help in removing the distraction.

Room Temperature

Ask that the room be cool, if possible. Comedian Steve Martin once said in an interview that audiences laugh more if they are a little cool. I recently told a story to the same fifth-grade class on two different days. On the first day, I began at 8:30 a.m., and the students roared with appreciation at my funny story. On the second day, I started at 12:45 p.m. The children had just had lunch, and it was very hot. I told a never-miss comic tale . . . and they listened politely with barely a smile.

On another occasion, I was performing at a school with the sweat running down my forehead into my eyes and my hair sticking to my neck. I had forgotten to bring a washcloth to wipe away the perspiration. I'm a plump person, so it's always 10 degrees hotter for me than for skinny people, and when I've got my adrenaline pumping for a performance, that seems to add another 10 degrees. Afterwards, the principal said blithely, "I guess we could have turned on the air conditioning."

Other Requirements

Explain to the booker exactly what you need well in advance and write it in your contract. Be prepared for inevitable changes. When I am spending a full day at a school, I ask for two 15-minute breaks and at least half an hour for lunch. I soon learned to specify that the 15 minutes between assemblies did not count as a break. Most assemblies are a little late in starting, and I always talk to the students at the end of the show. Some children linger for the full 15 minutes to tell me stories and ask me questions. I have to shoo them away as the classes for the next assembly start filing in. This leaves no time to check my makeup, comb my hair, locate the restroom, or take a breather before I begin the next set of stories.

I require bookers to mail me a written schedule of my visit at least one week in advance so that I can check it over and plan my presentations. Some do. Some don't. Sometimes the schedule is changed at the last minute, and I am only informed of the changes when I arrive.

I also ask if the booker will be providing me with meals, or if I'll need to arrange my own lunch. Most bookers are happy to feed me, but often they don't think to do so automatically.

I used to ask for a glass of water, but got tired of tiny paper cups filled with ice water, so I started bringing my own sports bottle filled with room-temperature bottled water.

If I need them for a workshop, I ask for access to a chalkboard *with* chalk and eraser (assume nothing!) or a white board with markers and eraser.

If I'm performing on a stage for a large audience, I ask that the house lights be left on or only dimmed a bit. Many years ago, at my first out-of-state storytelling festival, I blithely walked out on the stage and was immediately blinded by spotlights. The audience was a dark void into which I threw my story. I had assumed that everyone agreed that storytelling works best when the teller can look each listener in the face. Other tellers prefer the spotlight or request that only part of the stage be lit. What else do you want: a stool, a wireless microphone, or a room in which you can change into a costume and do your pre-show preparations? Tell your booker in advance.

Once I booked a storyteller into a coffeehouse. He inquired in advance if smoking was allowed, as he was allergic to cigarette smoke. It was a nonsmoking restaurant, so that was fine. What he forgot to ask, though, was whether there were candles on the tables. When he arrived and found them burning, he asked if they could be extinguished as even their smoke would bother him. Just the act of putting them out caused enough smoke to keep him up all night with itching eyes and a sore throat. He now requests that there be no candles as well as no smoking at any of his venues.

Prepare Your Audiences for a Show or Workshop

Story Rules

Sometimes, as I'm preparing to tell, I look at my audience and see toddlers running around, mothers or teachers gossiping, and other children and adults who are staring at me expectantly. Usually in this situation, the host has made a simple introduction that didn't mention what is required of an audience at a storytelling show. So I briefly review the "rules." I explain quickly that this will be "straight" storytelling with no props and that any children too young to understand should be taken out if they get noisy. I ask that any adults who wish to have a conversation do so in another room. Believe me, some listeners do need to be reminded of these basic rules and some may not abide by them even after you review them, but at least you will have tried.

Prepare the Teacher

If you're going to a preschool or elementary school, ask the teachers to tell their students that they should listen politely without interrupting, fidgeting, playing with the Velcro on their shoes, or other distracting behavior. To facilitate this, I always send a copy of the handout on page 28 to the principal three weeks before I perform and ask that it be photocopied for all the teachers.

Preparing Students for a Storytelling Experience

Imagination is a muscle that should be exercised. Students who can visualize an apple in their mind's eye when they hear the word will find it easier to comprehend the word *apple* when they read it on a page. When Albert Einstein was asked what preparation was needed to become a great scientist, he answered, "Read fairy tales." When asked what else to do, he responded, "Read more fairy tales." Please conduct the following imagination exercises with your class in preparation for the upcoming storytelling show.

Ask your class to close their eyes. Have them imagine a dragon. Tell them it's up to each person to decide what the dragon looks, feels, smells, moves, and sounds like. Explain that there is no wrong answer. After they have thought about it for a while, have the students open their eyes and share their answers.

Ask the students what they would wish for if they had only one wish—and it couldn't be for more wishes—and it had to be for someone else's benefit. Try not to be judgmental of their answers.

Talk to your class about the structure of stories. Tell them that every story has a beginning, a middle, and an end. Make sure that they know the difference between a story and a report. Read them a story about a whale. Then read them a short report on some basic facts about whales. Do not tell the class in advance which is the story and which is the report. See if they can figure out which is which.

Explain that telling a story is different than reading a story silently or out loud. Tell the students the beginning of a story. Then read them the story's middle. Finish by having them read the end silently to themselves. Have a discussion about how the three activities differed.

Be aware that the performance will be storytelling without props or pictures. If you believe that your students will be unable to sit still for a full 30-minute show, please let me know how long they can be attentive.

Discuss appropriate listening behavior with your class. This includes sitting quietly unless directed by the storyteller to participate; not playing with Velcro on shoes, lunch boxes, or each other; and applauding at the end of each story.

On the day of the storytelling presentation, have your class prepare by doing a favorite physical stretch or action rhyme. Have the students sit up straight in their chairs, close their eyes, and take three deep breaths to relax. You might have them walk to the performance space in silence and ask that they listen to all the sounds they hear on the way.

At the assembly, please seat near yourself any children who might misbehave so you can handle the problem unobtrusively.

The students look to you to model enthusiasm and interest. Please do not grade homework or talk during the presentation. If I ask for audience participation, I appreciate it when you also participate.

Thank you for your cooperation in preparing the students for the storytelling presentation. I'm sure that the students will enjoy it.

An excellent book on imagination exercises is *Put Your Mother on the Ceiling* by Richard De Mille (New York: Penguin Books, 1955).

Prepare the Performance Area
for a Show or Workshop

When you are planning a performance, ask how many seats are in the space where you will be presenting and how many bodies the booker expects at the event. If there will be significantly more seats than bodies, ask that the booker rope off the back rows so your audience won't scatter across the entire space.

You can do as veteran storyteller Caroline Bauer does and rope off areas yourself where you don't want people sitting, such as the sides or the back of a room.

However, this means getting there early. You should always be 30–60 minutes early for your gigs. Walk around the space. Can you close doors that lead to noisy areas? Do you need to pick up trash or move unsightly objects from your performance space?

Familiarize yourself with the microphones, sound systems, and lighting situations. It never fails that when you need assistance with such matters, no one else knows how to work the equipment either. If you do find someone at the site who knows what they're doing, have them show you so you'll be better informed the next time. Take a class in lighting and sound at a local college.

Show Up on Time

When planning when to leave for a gig, always allow time to get lost, deal with heavy traffic, find a parking space, check in, walk to the performance area, set up and test sound equipment, go to the restroom, check your makeup, warm up, and run through your stories again.

When I have a morning booking more than 60 miles from my home, I drive up the afternoon before and stay at a hotel or friend's home. Traffic in southern California is so bad that I wouldn't want to chance getting stuck in it and not arriving on time.

When I am going to give a presentation at a school, I always allow time to check in at the office and get directions to the classroom. This may require finding a pencil to sign their visitor's book and waiting for the busy secretary to answer my questions. Some school campuses are so big that it takes at least 10 minutes to walk to the classroom from the office.

Follow Up Bookings
with Thank-You Notes

People appreciate the courtesy of thank-you notes. You can also use the correspondence to mention other things you can do in future bookings. Plant the seed now. A sample note is included on page 30.

When students send me thank-you notes, I always reply and am sure to respond to any questions or requests.

Dear Director,

Thanks so much for asking me to tell stories to the children at your preschool. I hope they and your staff enjoyed it as much as I did.

The handouts I gave you can be copied for your staff and parents. This is a one-time permission.

I would appreciate a note from you on official stationery about what your staff liked about my show and what you would suggest that I change to improve it.

I have shows for Halloween, Christmas and Hanukkah, family gatherings, and even a special preschooler show called "Noises in the Night." I can do workshops for staff and/or parents on how to tell stories. I would be happy to work with you again.

Sincerely,

Harlynne Geisler

Stick to Your Artistic and Professional Standards

Many years ago, a museum asked me to do two shows for a laughably small amount of money. My mouth agreed, but I think my brain must not have, because I showed up at the wrong time for the first show. I did the second show, but returned the check with my apologies. I realized then that if I didn't listen to myself, I would subconsciously sabotage any show in which I wasn't living by my standards.

Be clear about what you are willing to be flexible about, and what issues on which you will not compromise. When a school asks you to do 10 classroom presentations in one day with no breaks and a 20-minute lunch, explain that you can only do four presentations in a day, because each requires a lot of energy, and the tenth class deserves as much from you as the first.

You make all future artists who stick to their standards look like prima donnas if you fold and do whatever the booker wants. So stand up for yourself and for your art!

Resources

Further Reading

De Mille, Richard. *Put Your Mother on the Ceiling*. New York: Penguin Books, 1955.

The introduction talks about the importance of imagination in education. The rest of the book tells how to do imagination games with students.

Chapter 4

Selling Storytelling

To market yourself as a storyteller, you may have to sell your potential employers on the importance of storytelling itself.

Little Money, Lots of Choices

There is competition for every dollar in your markets. The local PTA has to decide how much of the money it raises will go for assemblies and how much for other improvements such as playground equipment. The teacher has to decide whether to use the funds allocated for gifted student enrichment to bring in a presenter for one hour or buy a computer program that can be used every day. The parent has to decide whether to hire entertainment for a child's birthday party or buy a bigger birthday present. The church has to decide whether to have a performer as part of the service or buy a hot plate for the kitchen.

Even if these decision makers choose a performer for entertainment, enrichment, or enlightenment, they still have to decide which act, and there's plenty of competition. They could book an animal act for the assembly, a historian for the classroom, a clown for the party, or a gospel singer for the church.

In chapter 1, I briefly explained why storytelling is important and where it can be used. You can also promote storytelling to potential bookers by quoting some of the following experts.

Why Bother? The Experts Give Reasons for Telling Stories

Storytelling in Schools

Storytelling fits into almost every facet of school life. It teaches morals without preaching; encourages reading; and it devel-

ops relationships between the tellers and the listeners, whether it is a professional, the principal, or another staff member sharing a tale or students telling to other students. Storytelling can be used to explain science, history, social studies, and math. It helps develop creativity and imagination. But don't take just my word for it. Here's what others have said about storytelling.

Jean de La Fontaine (1621–1695)

Fables in sooth are not what they appear;
Our moralists are mice, and such small deer.
We yawn at sermons, but we gladly turn
To moral tales, and so amused we learn.

Abraham Lincoln (1809–1865)

They say I tell a great many stories; I reckon I do, but I have found in the course of a long experience that common people, take them as they run, are more easily informed through the medium of a broad illustration than in any other way, and as to what the hypercritical few may think, I don't care.

California Reading Association

Whereas all students benefit from the incorporation of storytelling in the curriculum, and whereas storytelling emphasizes the ties that bind the community of people together through universal commonalties which are found in stories from all over the world, and whereas students improve their ability to speak in front of others, and whereas students gain self-confidence, be it therefore resolved that the California Reading Association advocates that storytelling should be a part of the regular curriculum that every student experiences and that students should become active participants in the act and art of storytelling.[1]

California State Department of Education

Folklore exerts its appeal down through the ages and in widely separated cultures because it deals with the deepest human feelings and experiences. By reading the stories, children can enjoy the puzzles of good and evil, fear and courage, wisdom and folly, fortune and misfortune, cruelty and kindness. The tales help readers and listeners to explain the world and to bridge its confusing dimensions.[2]

United States Department of Education

Research Finding: Telling young children stories can motivate them to read. Storytelling also introduces them to cultural values and literary traditions before they can read, write, and talk about stories by themselves.

Comment: Elementary school teachers can introduce young students to the study of literature by telling them fairy tales such as the *Three Billy Goats Gruff* or *Beauty and the Beast* and myths such as *The Iliad*. Even students with low motivation and weak academic skills are more likely to listen, read, write, and work hard in the context of storytelling.

Stories from the oral tradition celebrate heroes who struggle to overcome great obstacles that threaten to defeat them. Children are neither bored nor alienated by learning literature through storytelling; they enjoy, understand, and sympathize naturally with the goats on the bridge, Beauty in a lonely castle, and Hector and Achilles outside the walls of Troy. With the help of skillful questioning, they can also learn to reflect on the deeper meanings of these stories.

Storytelling can ignite the imaginations of children, giving them a taste of where books can take them. The excitement of storytelling can make reading and learning fun and can instill in children a sense of wonder about life and learning.[3]

National Council of Teachers of English

Once upon a time, oral storytelling ruled. It was the medium through which people learned their history, settled their arguments, and came to make sense of the phenomena of their world. Then along came the written word with its mysterious symbols. For a while, only the rich and privileged had access to its wonders. But in time, books, signs, pamphlets, memos, cereal boxes, constitutions—countless kinds of writing appeared everywhere people turned. The ability to read and write now ruled many lands. Oral storytelling, like the simple-minded youngest brother in the olden tales, was foolishly cast aside. Oh, in casual ways people continued to tell each other stories at bedtime, across dinner tables, and around campfires, but the respect for storytelling as a tool of learning was almost forgotten.

Luckily, a few wise librarians, camp counselors, folklorists, and traditional tellers from cultures which still highly valued the oral tale kept storytelling alive. Schoolchildren at the feet of a storyteller sat mesmerized and remembered the stories till the teller came again. Teachers discovered that children could easily recall whatever historical or scientific facts they learned through story. Children realized they made pictures in their minds as they heard stories told, and they kept making pictures even as they read silently to themselves. Just hearing stories made children want to tell and write their own tales. Parents who wanted their children to have a sense of history found eager ears for the kind of story that begins, When I was little. . . . Stories, told simply from mouth to ear, once again traveled the land.

Why Include Storytelling in School? Everyone who can speak can tell stories. We tell them informally as we relate the mishaps and wonders of our day-to-day lives. We gesture, exaggerate our voices, pause for effect. Listeners lean in and compose the scene of our tale in their minds. Often they are likely to be reminded of a similar tale from their own lives. These naturally learned oral skills can be used and built on in our classrooms in many ways.

Students who search their memories for details about an event as they are telling it orally will later find those details easier to capture in writing. Writing theorists value the rehearsal, or prewriting, stage of composing. Sitting in a circle and swapping personal or fictional tales is one of the best ways to help writers rehearse.

Listeners encounter both familiar and new language patterns through story. They learn new words or new contexts for already familiar words. Those who regularly hear stories, subconsciously acquire familiarity with narrative patterns and begin to predict upcoming events. Both beginning and experienced readers call on their understanding of patterns as they tackle unfamiliar texts. Then they re-create those patterns in both oral and written compositions. Learners who regularly tell stories become aware of how an audience affects a telling, and they carry that awareness into their writing.

Both tellers and listeners find a reflecting of themselves in stories. Through the language of symbol, children and adults can act out through a story the fears and understandings not so easily expressed in everyday talk. Story characters represent the best and worst in humans. By exploring story territory orally, we explore ourselves—whether it be through ancient myths and folktales, literary short stories, modern picture books, or poems. Teachers who value a personal understanding of their students can learn much by noting what story a child chooses to tell and how that story is uniquely composed in the telling. Through this same process, teachers can learn a great deal about themselves.

Story is the best vehicle for passing on factual information. Historical figures and events linger in children's minds when communicated by way of a narrative. The ways of other cultures, both ancient and living, acquire honor in story. The facts about how plants and animals develop, how numbers work, or how government policy influences history—any topic, for that matter—can be incorporated into story form and made more memorable if the listener takes the story to heart.

Children at any level of schooling who do not feel as competent as their peers in reading or writing are often masterful at storytelling. The comfort zone of the oral tale can be the path by which they reach the written one. Tellers who become very familiar with even one tale by retelling it often, learn that literature carries new meaning with each new encounter. Students working in pairs or in small storytelling groups learn to negotiate the meaning of a tale.

How Do You Include Storytelling in School? Teachers who tell personal stories about their past or present lives model for students the way to recall sensory detail. Listeners can relate the most vivid images from the stories they have heard or tell back a memory the story evokes in them. They can be instructed to observe the natural storytelling taking place around them each day, noting how people use gesture and facial expression, body language, and variety in tone of voice to get the story across.

Stories can also be rehearsed. Again, the teacher's modeling of a prepared telling can introduce students to the techniques of eye contact, dramatic placement of a character within a scene, use of character voices, and more. If students spend time rehearsing a story, they become comfortable using a variety of techniques. However, it is important to remember that storytelling is communication, from the teller to the audience, not just acting or performing.

Storytellers can draft a story the same way writers draft. Audio tape or videotape recordings can offer the storyteller a chance to be reflective about the process of telling. Listeners can give feedback about where the telling engaged them most. Learning logs kept throughout a storytelling unit allow both teacher and students to write about the thinking that goes into choosing a story, mapping its scenes, coming to know its characters, deciding on detail to include or exclude.

Like writers, student storytellers learn from models. Teachers who tell personal stories or go through the process of learning to tell folk or literary tales make the most credible models. Visiting storytellers or professional tellers on audio tapes or videotapes offer students a variety of styles. Often a community historian or folklorist has a repertoire of local tales. Older students both learn and teach when they take their tales to younger audiences or community agencies. Once you get storytelling going, there is no telling where it will take you.

Oral storytelling is regaining its position of respect in communities where hundreds of people of every age gather together for festivals in celebration of its power. Schools and pre-service college courses are gradually giving it curriculum space as well. It is unsurpassed as a tool for learning about ourselves, about the ever-increasing information available to us, and about the thoughts and feelings of others.

The simpleminded youngest brother in olden tales, while disregarded for a while, won the treasure in the end every time. The NCTE Committee on Storytelling invites you to reach for a treasure—the riches of storytelling.[4]

What You Can Do in the Schools

Whole-school storytelling assemblies for holidays, awards, and other events can be very entertaining and effective. Another way to make sure that everyone in the school experiences your stories is to perform in one place and have one to three classes come to listen at a time. You can conduct workshops for students, staff, and parents on storytelling, history, folklore, creative writing, or related topics. You can be part of evening or weekend PTA events, multicultural fairs, or storytelling festivals with student performers, community tellers, and other freelance artists.

What You Can Do in Libraries

All those wonderful books, media, and periodicals will just sit on the shelves without patrons to check them out. An excellent way to draw patrons into the library is through special programs such as storytelling. Sometimes those programs will be conducted by staff members, sometimes by outside tellers. Once the patrons are in the library, use the stories as entertaining book talks to educate and interest them in library materials.

The library is all about providing literature and information to its patrons. Storytellers can do both—and not just for the children. Programs can be aimed at preschoolers, school-age children, families, adults, or seniors. I did a successful Bedtime Stories series at which children of ages three to seven were encouraged to come in pajamas with their favorite bedtime toy and at least one parent. The toys were always introduced to me and (with the child's permission) lined up near my chair so that they could listen to the stories too. Could the librarian have done the series herself? Yes, and she did, using puppets and picture books. But she was overworked and didn't have time to prepare tales by heart. She wanted the children to have the experience of listening and participating in oral literature and to enjoy a voice other than her own occasionally, so she hired me.

Summertime is when most public libraries try to lure young readers with programs. Call the children's services director during the winter to be on the mailing list of summer performers. Find out what the library's summer theme is so that you can research a program that fits. Then write a short description of your program that will be placed in the list along with your name, phone number, and fee.

With help, librarians can target any age. How about creating a workshop to encourage parents to tell to their preschoolers, a lecture to remind seniors to share memories with their relatives, or a festival in which adolescents tell to younger children? Suggest working with the staff to train them as tellers.

As a former librarian, I became a storyteller in part to take the literature to the streets. I still love to be surrounded by books when I tell. If the library has a written source for any stories I tell, I always mention them and try to display them on a nearby table to point to as I introduce the story. I even help children and adults find books on subjects that I mention during my shows. This is an extra service that the librarians appreciate.

Resources

Further Reading

For ideas on selling storytelling to other audiences, see:

Armstrong, David. *Managing by Storying Around: A New Method of Leadership.* New York: Doubleday, 1992.
How managers can do their jobs better by using storytelling.

Bettelheim, Bruno. *The Uses of Enchantment: The Meaning and Importance of Fairy Tales.* New York: Alfred A. Knopf, 1976.

Brett, Doris. *Annie Stories.* New York: Workman, 1988.

———. *More Annie Stories: Therapeutic Storytelling Techniques.* New York: Magination Press, 1992.

Campbell, Joseph. *The Hero with a Thousand Faces.* Princeton, NJ: Princeton University Press, 1968.

Greene, Ellin, and George Shannon. *Storytelling: A Selected Annotated Bibliography.* New York: Garland, 1986.
Besides the section "Purpose and Values of Storytelling," see the section "Storytelling in Special Settings or to Groups with Special Needs." By reading the recommended articles and books, you will learn more about how to tell and how to sell to young children, adolescents, seniors, handicapped, families, and outreach programs.

Keen, Sam, and Anne Valley-Fox. *Your Mythic Journey: Finding Meaning in Your Life Through Writing and Storytelling.* Los Angeles: Jeremy P. Tarcher, 1973, 1989.

McCutcheon, Priscilla, and Karen Tecott. *Developing Older Audiences: Guidelines for Performing Arts Groups.* Washington, DC: National Council on the Aging, 1985.
How to market to older adults. Lists additional resource materials. Can be ordered for $4 (which includes shipping) from the National Council on the Aging, Department 5087, Washington, DC 20061-5087.

Notes

1. The quotation on page 32 from *Recommended Readings in Literature, Kindergarten Through Grade Eight*, copyright 1986, is reprinted by permission of the California Department of Education, P.O. Box 271, Sacramento, CA 95812-0271.

2. California State Department of Education, *Recommended Readings in Literature: Kindergarten Through Grade Eight* (Burlingame, CA: California State Department of Education, 1987), 5.

3. United States Department of Education, *What Works: Research About Teaching and Learning* (Washington, DC: U.S. Department of Education, 1986), 25.

4. National Council of Teachers of English, "Teaching Storytelling: A Position Statement from the Committee on Storytelling." (Urbana, IL: National Council of Teachers of English, n.d.).

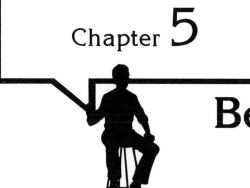

Chapter 5

Becoming Known and Being Remembered

One Rainy Night: An Urban Legend

Two young men were driving around downtown San Diego late one rainy night when they saw a girl standing on the corner of Broadway and First. She didn't have an umbrella or a raincoat. She was wearing a long, beautiful white gown, like a prom dress. She was soaking wet, and she looked lost.

Being nice fellows, the men stopped the car and said, "Miss, do you need a ride somewhere?" She said, "Yes," and explained that she was trying to get back to her mother's house. Then she got in the backseat of the car and gave them the address up in the Mission Hills area.

The two men started off, and the one who wasn't driving looked back at the girl. She was shivering in the backseat, the rain dripping off her, and he felt so sorry for her that he said, "Why don't you wear my coat till we get there? It will keep you warm." She thanked him and put the jacket on. They continued driving to the street she'd named and pulled up outside the house.

The one young man turned around to tell the girl they were there . . . and she wasn't!

There was nobody in the backseat. They hadn't heard the car door open or shut. They couldn't figure out what kind of a weird practical joke this was.

So they went up to the house and knocked, and a middle-aged woman came to the door. She seemed not to be surprised at being awakened at that time of night. She looked really sad. One of the two men said, "We're sorry to bother you so late, but we picked up a girl in a white dress downtown. She told us she lived here and was trying to get home, but when we pulled up outside your house, she wasn't in the back of our car."

The woman knew right away what they were talking about. She said, "That was my daughter. Five years ago she and her boyfriend were on their way home from a school dance. Their car skidded on a rainy road, and they were both killed in the crash."

"Ever since then, every year on the anniversary of her death, she reappears on the spot where they died. Some kind soul always picks her up, but when they get to my house, she's vanished from the car."

Now these were two very contemporary young guys, and they just didn't believe this at all. They said, "We're sorry. It's not that we think that you're lying or anything, but that's ridiculous. We don't believe in ghosts."

The woman replied, "If you don't think I'm telling the truth, just go down two blocks and turn right. You'll see the cemetery up ahead. Go in there, and on the left, under an oak tree, you'll find her grave." She told them the name of her daughter and showed them a photograph of the very girl they'd picked up.

So they went down the two blocks, turned to the right, went in the cemetery, and under the oak tree was the young woman's grave.

And the borrowed coat was lying across the headstone.

The End 📖

There are many versions of the urban legend "One Rainy Night." It is usually titled "The Vanishing Hitchhiker." Some of the other versions are listed in the "Resources" section at the end of this chapter. Several tellers use this tale as one of their signature stories. A signature story is one that becomes identified with the performer because they have made it their own.

You might call this my signature written story. When newspapers ask me for a story to print in an article about me or about spooky stories in general, I give them this one and change the locations in the story to local landmarks. I don't give them an actual signature story that I'll be using at the concert that they're publicizing because I want the stories that I tell to be a surprise to my audience. When the *Desert Sun* printed this story in an article publicizing "Delicious Shivers," a dinner show I was doing at a Palm Springs health spa, the spa sold out the show.

Establishing Your Niche

What Type of Stories Do You Wish to Be Known For?

Decide on what type of stories you'd like to focus on to begin with—folktales, myths, short stories, original tales, biographies, history, personal stories, and so on—you can always broaden your repertoire later. You can tell stories that come from your own cultural background, from a culture that you've spent a lot of time with, or a culture that you wish to research. Sometimes your stories will be dictated by the season, such as ghost stories for Halloween, or by the booker. I spent the summer of 1995 telling tales about dogs because the summer reading club topic for the southern California public libraries was "Paws to Read." Sometimes the stories will be part of your identity. For example, you may wish to become known as a religious storyteller who shares Bible tales in contemporary language.

What Audiences Do You Want to Be Known By?

Do you want to target a particular age group? Where will you tell to them? For example, if you prefer telling to preschoolers, you can perform at day-care centers, bookstores, community centers, libraries, religious institutions, parties, and children's festivals. If you'd rather work with seniors, you could still meet with them at bookstores, community centers, libraries, religious institutions, and parties, but you can also perform at senior centers, retirement homes, convalescent hospitals, and adult education venues.

As I wrote in chapter 1, research your market. Find out what is important to your potential audience. This will help you choose stories that are right for your listeners and help you present them in a way they can appreciate and understand.

What Is Your Name?

Whenever someone meeting me for the first time says, "Harlynne Geisler? I've heard your name before," I know that my private publicity campaign is working. I want my name to be out there in so many places that people will assume that I must be a great storyteller—otherwise why would everyone be talking about me? Of course, I also hope that when they hear me in person, they won't be disappointed. You, too, will want your name out there where potential bookers will become familiar with it.

First you must decide how to describe yourself. Do you shy away from the term "storyteller," which is somewhat vague and used to describe everything from librarians reading books out loud to filmmakers to authors. People will often ask you what *you* mean by the term. If you plan to work mainly with business types, you might prefer to call yourself an "oral communicator" because the traditional term "storytelling" is associated in most people's minds with performing for children.

Do you wish to use your own name, or will you make up a "stage name," as many performers do? There are already tellers and telling duos with names such as Kathlyn the Great . . . Storyteller; The Tale-Teller; Deja-Views; Storytellers Two; Imagine That! Storytellers; the Purple Lady; the Legend Lady; the Story Lady; the Folktellers; the Storycrafters; Tellalore; Chartered Voyages Storytelling; Brother Blue; Angela the Yarnspinner; WiseTales; Jack's Mama; the Storytelling Clown; Grandpa Jim; Al Talking Moon; and Eth-Noh-Tec. If you plan to use a name other than your legal one for performances, ask your bank for a Fictitious Name statement, so you will be able to cash checks made out to your stage name.

When you choose a name, try to make sure it's not similar to that used by someone else who performs in the same area. For example, if the Legend Lady and the Story Lady both tell stories in Tucson retirement homes, people might call the Legend Lady when they mean to book the Story Lady.

Once you choose a name, make sure you use it everywhere. Put it on your checks. Announce it on your answering machine. Write it into your contract, and specify that it must be used in all publicity regarding your shows. If you wish, you can pay to be listed in the phone book under your name as a business.

Later you may decide to change your business name if it no longer suits you. Don't change it too often, though, as each change will make it harder to develop an identity that people remember.

Promotional Materials

Business Cards

Your business card is the first thing you should invest in. Business cards are small and easy to carry around, so they're less likely to be discarded than your brochures and press kits.

Your card should have the word "Storyteller" or whatever term you are using, your stage name, your name (if appropriate), your phone number, and an address (this can be a post office box). Make the card stands out with colored inks or papers, a logo or other graphic, and some information about what storytelling is or what your skills are. Look at other performers' business cards to get ideas.

Because I want potential bookers to know that I am not just a children's performer, my card says "shows for all ages & occasions" and "workshops & lectures" printed above my phone number in the bottom right corner.

Once you've got a card, use it. Give it out to anyone who might be interested in your services. My husband carries a couple with him so he can give them out. Include your card when you're handing out or mailing brochures or fliers. Post them on public bulletin boards, give them to your friends to pass on, stack them on tables at events, hand them to everyone you meet—why, even your grocery store clerk might be thinking of a storyteller for her child's birthday party!

Stationery

Appearance in business is important. Stationery on nice paper stock with a logo that matches your cards and brochures tells potential bookers that you are a professional performer, and a professional can demand higher compensation than an amateur.

My first stationery was printed on paper similar to my business cards and brochures. The heading "Storyteller Harlynne Geisler" was in the same typeface and ink color as both my brochure and stationery. When people saw the beige paper, blue ink, and heading, I wanted them to think of me before they read any further.

I now print many of my letters on my computer printer, but always make a nice letterhead.

Brochures

Brochures introduce you to people who have never met you and tell people who have met you more about you and your services. A brochure should include a picture of you, explain what you can do for a booker, and outline your experience. These are all questions a potential booker would ask.

I believe that it's better to have a simple business card than to put out an amateurish brochure. I purchased a computer program for creating brochures, but found designing my own brochure too difficult. Eventually, I invested in a professionally designed brochure, and now feel it was one of my wisest investments. A good brochure can last you a decade, as mine has. I continue to use the format and photos, but I have my printer update the specific information each time I reprint it.

When designing or planning your brochure, pick up several at a storytelling festival or meeting. Look at each with a critical eye. What do you like and dislike about them? What tips you off that a person doesn't have much experience? One thing I always notice is amateurish photographs. Hire a professional to shoot you while telling stories in more than one place and in more than one outfit. Be sure to get permission to use the photo for other publicity purposes. Whenever people take photos of me, I ask that they send me copies and offer to reimburse them. Even an amateur can get a great shot that you may use.

Samuel Patrick Smith in "The Professional Edge" column in *Laugh Makers* explains about how to use typography to sell your services, crop photos for maximum effect, and write copy that includes a "call to action."[1] Check out your library for books on creating brochures.

No matter who designs the brochure, have at least two people you trust critique it and proofread the final draft before getting it printed. I did not proofread my final draft as carefully as I should have, though the printer asked me to read and approve the copy, so I ended up with 2,000 brochures that had incorrect information and places where bold print was used instead of italics. Only people reading every bit of the brochure carefully will notice these subtle mistakes, but they are glaring to me.

Fliers

I use fliers to supplement my brochure and to target specific audiences. When I spoke at a reading conference, I put out my brochure and a flier targeted to teachers that told some of the places I'd performed, listed my shows and workshops for schools, included quotations from principals and teachers on how effective and entertaining my school programs were, and listed my address and phone number. Because fliers are less expensive to produce than a brochure, it is easy to create a flier for a specific event or audience. Combined with the more complete brochure, an effective flier can give a specific target audience all the information they need about my services.

Designing Your Flier

People's eyes are drawn first to illustrations then to the copy. Make your flier look as professional and attractive as possible. Libraries Unlimited and Dover Publications publish many clip art books you can use to design fliers. The illustrations are copyright free.

There are books of clip art for libraries; of borders; of alphabets; and of humorous, romantic, or holiday illustrations. Book or commercial art stores often carry these books. There are several computer programs to help you design and illustrate fliers. I like the Print Shop Deluxe program.

Advertisements

A print advertisement can reach thousands of readers, but it must compete for their attention with all the other ads, articles, and photographs in a periodical. Ads are not cheap, so decide what your budget is and who you wish to target. If you're aiming for the birthday party crowd, a local parent's magazine would reach them and have the bonus of being read by many in the PTA, too. If you want to travel across the country with a show on Bible stories, consider an ad in a religious publication that goes to the denomination you are most interested in. An ad in a newspaper can help you fill the seats at a show.

Whether you're creating an ad for a publication or a flier advertising yourself or an event, put most of your thought and time into writing and designing the headline. You have only a few seconds of any reader's time. If the headline doesn't grab a person, she or he will throw your flier in the trash or turn the page. Just think about all the ads you see each day. You don't read each one. You focus on the ones that are of interest to you. Remember, your interests may not be the same as those of your potential bookers. Target them by creating copy that tells them why they should care about your services. What's in it for them? Keep your copy succinct, with lots of blank space rather than trying to fill every inch with words and pictures, which can make the ad look crowded.

Ads, like direct mailings, have more effect if they are repeated. Most publications give a discount for ads that appear in several issues. It is best to repeat your ad at least three times, so that people will start to notice it. Look at other ads in the publication you are choosing. What ads make you want to respond? Why? Model your ads on what works.

Research books on ads, take classes in advertising, and talk to the experts, possibly hiring them to create your ad.

You can cut down on your cost by using "remnant space." Magazines that have not sold all their ad space immediately prior to press time will sometimes sell the remnant spaces at a discount to fill their pages. Call publications you are interested in to ask what their policies are. You can also save money by placing ads only in the newspaper section that goes to a particular area or in a regional edition of a magazine.

Signs

I have a very unusual name. When it is pronounced (or mispronounced) during an introduction, I doubt if most listeners can imagine how it is correctly spelled. Because name recognition is an important part of public relations, I always pronounce my name correctly if it has been mangled by my emcee. If I have handouts for a show or workshop, my name and phone number is on every page so that if the copyright notice is ignored and the handout is distributed to others, at least my name will be before the readers.

I also want my name and its spelling to be remembered so future bookers can find it in the phone book. With this in mind I went to a sign store and ordered a bright blue, acrylic, 18-x-24-inch sign that reads: "Storyteller Harlynne Geisler" that I display when telling.

I feel much more professional having a sign announcing me. It tells students what to expect from me and prepares them to listen.

I once performed in a toy store after an Easter egg hunt. During the hunt itself, I put my sign out where I was to stand and retreated to the back office to be out of the way of the children. The owner came to get me when it was time for the show, saying, "The kids knew right where to sit when they were ready to listen. They're gathered in front of your sign."

I know that name recognition pays off as people have stopped mistaking me for the black-haired librarian and the gray-haired grandmother who also tell in my area. They see my red hair, multicolored glasses, story bag, and that bright blue sign, and they remember "Storyteller Harlynne Geisler."

Mailings to Potential Bookers

If you want to tell to schools, get a directory of the schools in the area and send them your brochure, a form letter explaining your services (assemblies, workshops, etc.) and prices, and letters of recommendations from other schools. A sample flier is on page 43 that I have sent to local schools along with my brochure and a cover letter.

In deciding on my fees for school assemblies in my town, I charge nothing for the third assembly. This is because while most schools in San Diego County choose to only have two assemblies due to lack of funds, I want to encourage them to have me tell to smaller groups. If a program chairperson protests that they don't have enough money to book me for even the two assemblies, I suggest that they find another school willing to share me. If two schools book me for the same day, it only costs $215 for each school to have two assemblies.

When I am giving a performance in an area where I am not known, I send a letter to other potential bookers in the area inviting them to preview my show (with the permission of my booker). I give the day, date, time, location, address, booker, and phone number for information for that show. I suggest that they call the booker after my show for a recommendation. As my colleague Heather Forest says, "Do your best, and word of mouth will do the rest."

Be warned, though. Direct mailing can be expensive. Postcards aren't cheap, once you add in the cost of stamps and printing, and the first couple of mailings might not generate a big response. Direct mailers consider a 7 percent response to a mailing a big success. You're more likely to get a 2 to 5 percent response. In other words, 1,000 postcards might land you only 20 warm bodies. That's show biz. Be sure to factor in the cost of the publicity when you are deciding how much to charge for an event.

There are two main reasons for direct mailing: 1) it reminds everyone of your name and phone number; and 2) it lets them know that you are still performing. I often get calls from bookers who sound surprised that I am still available as a storyteller 10 years after they first hired me.

You can purchase mailing lists for schools in any area of the United States directly from the school district or from mailing list companies (see the "Resources" section at the end of this chapter for addresses). The same would hold true for public libraries, churches, retirement homes, preschools, and so on. If you wish to tell at storytelling events in other areas, buy the National Storytelling Association's directory, which lists the events and their addresses. You can also obtain addresses of libraries, museums, day-care centers, private schools, children's camps, and so on by using online or CD-ROM directories, magazines and journals, and mailing list companies.

It is also important to start compiling your own mailing list. One way that I have built up my mailing list is to pass out evaluation forms at my workshops that include a space for people to write their names and addresses if they wish to receive a free copy of my newsletter. Everyone loves freebies, so people fill out that section. Then, when you plan shows or workshops that are open to the public, you can invite these people.

Storyteller Harlynne Geisler

There are a variety of storytelling themes and services your school can choose from, including:

- *Multicultural Tales from the Story Bag*: These stories from around the world include participatory tales for the younger students and longer, exciting tales for older students.

- *Spooky Stories*: This program is appropriate for Halloween but popular year round. Stories for the younger students are either funny or only mildly scary and often involve audience participation, while tales for the older children are a bit spookier.

- *Holiday Tales*: These non-religious Christmas and Hanukkah stories are available in two shows—one for older students and one for younger students.

- *A Full-Day Visit*: Start with assemblies. Then Harlynne will spend time with selected classes, teaching them student storytelling or leading creative writing exercises. Ask for further information about this program.

Additional services include:

- *With Every Booking a Bonus*: Your school will receive a packet of several suggested classroom activities and bibliographies of recommended books and tapes to follow up Harlynne's visit and tie storytelling into the curriculum.

- *Workshops for Parents, Teachers, Librarians, and/or Students*: Harlynne has several workshops to choose from, or she can tailor a workshop to meet your group's specific needs.

Fees:

- $185 First Assembly
- $160 Second Assembly
- FREE Third Assembly
- $85 Each Additional Assembly on the same day within the same school district
- $550 Full-Day Visit/Visit to School Outside of San Diego County (plus expenses)
- $150 Per Hour of Storytelling Workshop
- 20% Off for Schools with an Enrollment of under 400 Students

These prices are valid from 9/95–6/96, so act today!

Call: Storyteller Harlynne Geisler
c/o *Story Bag: A National Storytelling Newsletter*
5361 Javier Street
San Diego, CA 92117-3215
(619) 569-9399

If You Move

If you change your address or phone number, be sure to notify everyone on your mailing list. Fill out a change of address notice at the post office, then check every three to six months to see whether your forwarding order has expired by sending yourself a letter to your old address. If the order has expired, fill out another change of address notice at the post office, putting the day you are filling out the new notice as your moving date. You must make it as easy as possible for people to find you.

Most post offices will not let you continue to do this forever, so you may have to explain the circumstances. The manager at my old post office agreed to continue forwarding mail to me five years after I'd moved because I explained that a new book had listed my old address as the place to write for my information packet.

The post office does not charge for this service. Alas, the phone company charges for almost everything. For a limited time, the phone company will notify callers dialing your old number of your new phone number. Eventually, though, they will reassign the old number to someone else. Call your old number every month. When instead of hearing a recording announcing your new phone number, you find yourself speaking to the new owner of your old number, ask if that person will be kind enough to tell people who call looking for you what your new number is. If you choose, you can pay a monthly fee to have your old number never given to anyone else. Instead the phone company will automatically switch anyone dialing your old number to your new phone number. Of course, whenever possible keep your old number, so your older promotional materials remain current.

The Media

Press Releases

Do you have something to crow about? Be sure to crow to the press! A good way to circulate news about yourself as a storyteller is to send press releases to the media. Have you won an award, created a new show, begun your business, or started a storytelling group? Anything can be newsworthy, especially to the smaller papers in your community.

When I performed at a school in a small town north of Los Angeles, the PTA president called the local newspaper. The fact that I'd come the 180 miles from San Diego to spend the day at the school telling and teaching was considered newsworthy by the hometown paper. They sent a reporter to interview me and a photographer to snap my picture.

There are many books at the library that can teach you the art of an effective press release and publicity campaign (I'm assuming you are not rich enough to hire your own publicity agent). When you read the newspaper, ask yourself, "What was the angle that got that person published in the paper?" Then apply that knowledge towards getting yourself in the paper.

When writing your article, be sure to clearly label it "Press Release"; include your name, address, and phone number so that a reporter can contact you for further information; create a headline; and limit your information to one page with double-spaced lines. Write short sentences with lots of action verbs, and make sure the spelling and grammar are correct. When sending the release, address it to the attention of the person in charge of calendar listings or feature articles. If you don't know that person's name, call the periodical to find out. Some people suggest that you deliver the press release in person with something to grab the reporter's attention, such as a T-shirt advertising the festival, a jack-o'-lantern to announce your Halloween show, balloons with your name and the name of the award you've won printed on them, and so on. Also, be sure to include invitations and free tickets to all your shows and any giveaways you've created to promote yourself.

Here is a press release that I used for several shows at different locations, changing the information on date, time, and place for each show.

PRESS RELEASE

Story Bag: A National Storytelling Newsletter
5361 Javier Street
San Diego, CA 92117-3215
Contact: Harlynne Geisler
Ph: 619-569-9399

FOR IMMEDIATE RELEASE

Woof! There It Is . . . At ABC Bookstore

Lassie, Spot, and Rin Tin Tin are just some of the famous dogs we all know, but dogs have been celebrated since long before books and movies came along. Every country has folktales of heroic dogs and superstitions that explain how dogs can be good or bad luck. Storyteller Harlynne Geisler will share tales that celebrate human's best friend in a free program for families called "Woof! Dog Tales Around the World" at ABC Bookstore, One Street, San Diego, on Tuesday, September 12, 1995, at 7:00 p.m. For further information, call ABC Bookstore at 555-8011.

Harlynne Geisler has performed all over San Diego County from Shamu Stadium to Reuben H. Fleet Space Center to the International Children's Festival as well as telling stories in 11 other states, Canada, and Mexico. Her book *Storytelling Professionally: The Nuts and Bolts of Becoming a Working Performer* will be published in 1997 by Libraries Unlimited.

This press release led to articles with photographs of me in newspapers in two different cities.

Press Kits

Press kits are for the more experienced storyteller. They can include photocopies of articles about you, résumés, press releases, and photos. It is an excellent idea to get two black-and-white photographs—a head shot and an action shot—taken by a professional photographer. Ask other performers who they have used. Get at least 100 5-x-7-inch prints of each pose. Send a photo with all advertising or promotional materials and press releases.

I find it useful to keep my name before the national storytelling community, so I send press releases about my upcoming shows to storytelling newsletters and magazines. I also send them to the newsletters of other organizations I belong to, such as the local writers' and editors' guild.

Interviews

I devote much of this chapter to media coverage. A positive article in a periodical or good coverage on a television or radio show will reach a larger audience than any mailing and influence more people than your ads. More importantly, it won't cost you a cent!

Ninety-nine percent of the time, what is said and written about storytellers and storytelling in the media is positive. However, it might be condescending, as many uninformed reporters think storytelling is only for small children, and the article won't appear in the theater section of the paper nor be treated as a high art form. Folk arts like storytelling are usually relegated to the Lifestyle section of the paper, magazine, or news show.

You will probably be asked the same questions by every reporter: What is storytelling? How did you get started? Where do you tell? What age is your favorite audience? How do you remember your stories? Where do you find tales to tell? and so on. This may seem tiresome, but it is an excellent opportunity to educate the public about what you can do.

I've had the good fortune to have had at least 45 interviews and photographs in newspapers and magazines, more than six television interviews, plus eight radio interviews. While there are many books and classes you can learn from, here's what I've learned from direct experience:

1. You are never off the record.

During a long-distance telephone interview, a newspaper reporter asked what I charge for my storytelling. I told him that I preferred to answer that off the record. Silly me. My reply was printed in the article. Ironically, that paper was the only one that has ever sent me a copy of the article stapled to a questionnaire asking whether everything printed in the article was accurate.

My policy is to never anger the media. I answered the questionnaire without mentioning the off-the-record comment. It was only a minor infraction. Years later when I performed again in that town, I was interviewed again. The reporter was different, but if I'd had the same reporter and had gotten him in trouble with his editor, he might not have written as positive a piece about me the second time.

2. What you say may be distorted, misquoted, and edited.

I try to take anything I learn from the media with a grain of salt. I am usually interviewed by reporters armed only with their faulty memories and a notebook. They remember the gist of what I said, but when they write it up for the paper, they're often not using my exact words. Because no reporter has taken the time to research storytelling before interviewing me, I find that their uninformed reworking of my comments sometimes changes the meaning. If they do it to me, I'm sure they do it to others about whom I read in the paper.

Even if the reporter gets it right, the editor may change the meaning by cutting the article to fit the space in the periodical. Fourteen years ago I was taken out to breakfast by a reporter. I told this reporter that I wanted to be considered for a special festival in Washington, D.C., but because the director was looking for representatives of all cultures, I wasn't sure if I'd be chosen. Jokingly I said, "I'm a 31-year-old Jewish-American woman from southern California. Do you think I have a chance?"

When I read the printed article, there was no mention of the fact that I was a professional freelance teller or that I was being considered for this important event. Instead, the article said, "Harlynne Geisler describes herself as a 31-year-old Jewish-American woman from southern California." It made me sound like an insignificant club woman. If the reporter had asked me to describe myself, I would not have used the words he took from my joking comment.

3. Talk nicely to media people.

Sticking to my policy of never getting angry at media, I called the reporter from the previous interview and asked him about the paragraph. He explained that all mention of the festival was edited out because of space. I told him that I had hoped to use comments from the article about the stories he had heard me tell at an evening performance. I asked politely if he could write me a letter on the newspaper's letterhead.

He sent me a glowing recommendation of my talent. I used a quote from that letter in my next brochure. Under the quote I put the reporter's name and the name of the newspaper.

In another instance, a big newspaper decided to cover a storytelling performance at a coffeehouse. One of the other tellers complained to the photographer that she couldn't concentrate with his lights shining in her face and that it was distracting to the listeners. He very politely stopped taking pictures of her. No photos of her ended up in the article.

I took a different approach. I let the photographer take pictures of me, and after the show, I thanked him for coming and asked for his card. I asked for copies of the photos he'd taken of me. He took my card and sent me copies of the three marvelous photos of me that were used with the article.

Television cameras and their lights are even more intrusive than photographers during a kids' show. I never tell children that a newspaper photographer is taking the pictures until after the show is over. Then I announce which paper they should read to look for their photos. But it's hard to ignore the television station logo blazoned across a video camera, and some children excited at the thought of being on television cause problems during a show. Try working with the reporters to solve the problem. One helpful reporter announced to the kids that if they were caught watching the camera instead of me, their faces wouldn't appear on television that evening. It worked.

Be nice to the media, and they will be (reasonably) nice to you.

4. Keep it short and positive.

Even when answering the same old questions for the umpteenth time, I still try to sound upbeat. One reporter wrote, "Geisler answers every question with a twinkle in her eye and a degree of enthu-

siasm that is usually reserved for teenagers in love."

Another wrote, "Listening to Harlynne Geisler, you get the impression that she would have loved to be in Alice's shoes when she tumbled into Wonderland."

It's doubly important to sound enthusiastic when being interviewed for radio or television. People should hear your voice and think, "That teller sounds so pleasant, I'd like to hear her in person."

Keep your replies short and snappy. Your interview may end up being only 20 or 30 seconds of air time. If they ask you to tell a story, choose a short one suitable for all ages.

5. Shape the truth you wish to share.

When I'm plugging an adult show, I don't always mention that I used to be an elementary school librarian, as some people will think I won't know how to perform for adults. In those cases, when a reporter asks for my personal history, I talk about belonging to a political theater group, my acting classes at University of California, San Diego, and my time with a private drama coach.

When you talk to a reporter, tell "the storyteller's truth" rather than all the straight facts. Choose wisely what and how much you wish to share about yourself, your life, and your work.

6. Get that business card.

Be sure to get the card of the reporter and photographer, and ask for copies of any photographs taken. The paper may charge a fee for photos, and many photographers are too busy to return your phone calls or send the photographs they promise. But keep asking. As with my experience with the wonderful photographer at the coffeehouse, sometimes it can really pay off.

Always write a note thanking the reporter and photographer for the interview, articles, and photographs. You can pitch other story ideas about yourself in this note.

Remember when dealing with the media that you are working together to inform the public about storytelling in general and yourself in particular. Be as cooperative as possible; the benefits in publicizing yourself can be enormous.

Articles and Letters to the Editor

Writing articles and letters to the editor about storytelling and related topics can be great free publicity (remember to identify yourself as a storyteller). I've had articles published on seniors telling to their grandchildren (for senior periodicals), on creating a love story for your sweetheart on Valentine's Day (for a local free newspaper), on finding out that I was a member of a Scottish clan (for my clan's international magazine), and bibliographies of good books to give children at holidays (for parenting magazines).

In-Person Promotions

Showcases and Booths

Ask your local PTA if they attend any showcases to preview assembly performers. If so, call the organizer for further information. Some conferences do not have showcases but do have booths that can be rented. Once I paid $500 for a booth at a PTA conference, from which I got two $500 bookings.

Make your booth or table look inviting. Use a tablecloth and skirt that complements your signs and brochures. Bring straight pins, tape, magic markers, your mailing list, pens, a sign that says "The Storyteller will be back in 10 minutes," plenty of water, and lunch.

Have a freebie to hand out. Candy is fine, but it's nicer if it's something with your name and phone number on it (see the "Giveaways" section later in this chapter). Be visible. Stand up, smile, and tell jokes. Ask in a friendly way if the people you meet would like a brochure. Don't take it personally when you see people scurrying by, trying not to make eye contact. If you have a chance to tell a story, keep it short and prepare a story that will appeal to adults as well as children.

Booking Conferences

Booking conferences are huge affairs with big-name stars and talent agents competing for bookings at colleges and theaters. It can be a daunting and expensive experience. In addition, it can take years of attendance to develop relationships with the bookers. When I took part in the Western Artists Alliance conference, they sent me a note warning all of us first-timers that it was very unlikely that we would get any bookings that year. I didn't get any. You should plan on attending for at least five years before getting booked. Because of the expense involved, booking conferences should only be considered by experienced, highly talented performers with strong egos.

See the appendix for a list of booking conferences and showcase opportunities.

Membership in Organizations

National Storytelling Association

You will probably want to join the National Storytelling Association (formerly NAPPS). Membership in the NSA looks good professionally, and you can be listed in the organization's *National Storytelling Directory*. While the *Directory* doesn't necessarily lead directly to bookings—I have been listed for 10 years and never received a single booking from it—it provides storytellers with contacts. If you plan to travel, write to local tellers and see if you can meet with them and maybe even get their assistance finding bookings. Remember, though, most tellers are not looking to give you their hard-earned bookings. When people call me and ask how to get bookings in my city, my first thought is, "I wish I knew!" Then I pass them on to people in town who might be able to help them. You might offer to give local tellers 10 percent of any fees that they can get you. They deserve to be paid for their hard work. The *Directory* also helps bookers who have heard you at big festivals find you more easily.

Another group you might wish to join is the National Story League, a service organization.

Local Storytelling Organizations

Belonging to a storytelling group can provide you with many benefits. These include the following:

- You'll meet good people.

- You'll hear wonderful stories.

- You'll get a chance to practice your own telling.

- You'll be taken more seriously by others because of being a member (and perhaps organizer or officer) of such a group.

- You may get storytelling jobs from people who hear you at group meetings.

Write to the National Storytelling Association to find out about storytelling groups and other freelance tellers in your area. If you find there are none, start your own, but be aware that it requires time and effort. Find a free room somewhere, and set a date at least a month in advance of the meeting. Send a press release about the meeting to every magazine, newspaper, television, and radio station in the area. Post an attractive flier about the meeting in every library, college, school, museum, and bookstore. Call every professional and amateur storyteller you know and every storytelling teacher, children's performer, folklorist, and other potentially interested persons you can find listed in adult education and college catalogs, phone books, and through local schools and libraries. Listeners will be the largest portion of your group—and what would the tellers be without them?

Be sure to have at least three tellers lined up in advance to tell at each meeting, and also invite impromptu performances. Limit the time each person has on the stage, or you'll have a microphone hog with a 30-minute tale take over. Don't charge for memberships or for participating in meetings, and don't attempt a newsletter until you have a proven interest.

Be aware as the goals of your organization are set that there may be conflicts among members. It's human nature.

Educational Organizations

There are associations to promote and support reading, libraries, literacy, teachers of all subjects, listening, and whole language programs, to name just a few. These associations have national conventions as well as regional and local meetings at which you can network and possibly line up jobs. If you present at one of these workshops, you probably won't be paid, but it can lead to other bookings. Your workshop should not be one long commercial about yourself, but you can talk about being a professional storyteller if it is an appropriate part of your lecture. Put your brochure on the table at the back of your workshop space or on everyone's chairs before they arrive.

Business Groups

Going to the monthly business meetings of the local chamber of commerce or other organization or attending community mixers can help you get bookings and find other business people to work with. These business meetings can also provide resources and contacts to help you run your business more effectively. Write to the national headquarters of these groups to find out about the local chapters. (See the appendix for the addresses.)

Less Familiar Publicity Routes

Word of Mouth

Anyone can lead to a booking, so you want everyone to know you are a storyteller. You may need to educate your friends, neighbors, and family members one-on-one about exactly what it is you do, then send them into the community to spread the word about your services. Sometimes you will have to answer the same questions again and again: "What's a storyteller?" "Where do you read to the kids?" "How did you get started?" "How do you remember your stories?" "Where do you find stories?" and so on. Try to come up with short, memorable answers to these questions. Give a "sample" of your skill by telling a 30-second story.

Incentives

A magician once gave me some of his business cards and told me that if I recommended him for a private party, he would give me 10 percent of his fee. You, too, can offer incentives to encourage people to recommend you. Some of the incentives I use include free subscriptions to my storytelling newsletter and movie tickets. Even your own mother might work harder for you if she knows that you'll take her out to dinner as reward for a booking.

Bumper Stickers

I have had bumper stickers that read "Support Your Local Storyteller" "Storyteller on Board" and "Tell me a story"—the latter sometimes led to young male jokesters pulling up beside me in traffic and shouting "Once upon a time . . . ." You can find bumper stickers at conferences or design your own. You might even print them up and give them away. The Oriental Trading Company prints custom bumper stickers. (See the address in the "Resources" section at the end of the chapter.)

Giveaways

Other promotional giveaways include balloons, pom-poms, sun visors, ribbons, plastic tumblers, sports bottles, pocket mirrors, key rings, pencils, notepads, stickers, and refrigerator magnets. These can be imprinted with your logo, name, phone number, and perhaps a cute saying. I prefer giveaways that can last forever, rather than items such as notepads that get used up, but whatever you choose, these gifts can help keep your name in front of your customer. I've listed the addresses of some mail-order companies in the "Resources" section at the end of this chapter, but also check your yellow pages for local companies. Shop around for price and quality.

Checks

I have the word "storyteller" printed on my checks above my name. People notice and question me about my profession. I always carry business cards and fliers about upcoming shows or workshops in my purse so that I can hand them out to anyone who seems interested after reading my check (or my T-shirt).

Answering Machine Messages

Your answering machine message should be a mini-audition. Here are two examples:

- One upon a time an evil wizard put (your name) under a magic spell that kept her from answering her telephone. Only you can break the spell's power. How? By waiting for the beep and leaving your name, phone number, and a message.

- Once upon a time (your name) was in her office. However, time passed, and she left on an adventure. If you would like to hear her story when she returns, leave your name, phone number, and a brief message at the sound of the tone.

Whatever message you use, keep it short! Few people today wish to listen to a message longer than 20 seconds. This applies as well to people receiving messages, so when leaving a message on a machine or with a person, briefly state your name, phone number, reason for calling, and the best times to reach you. No one likes to play phone tag, and if you are going to be in and out of your office, it helps the caller to know when they have the best chance of speaking to the real, live you.

On the Phone

You want to sound professional when people call. Potential bookers are expecting to speak to a businessperson, so when I say, "Hello, Storyteller Harlynne Geisler speaking," it prevents the awkward question of whether the caller has reached the right person. The caller also doesn't have to guess at the pronunciation of my name because I've just said it correctly. Anything that makes the conversation easier for the booker makes it more likely you will be hired.

One day I was speaking to a school principal on the phone, and she praised a colleague of mine, Martha Holloway, for being warm and personable in her phone conversa-

tions. I realized then that I was sometimes abrupt on the phone.

I bought a small mirror and put it on my desk. When I was on the phone, I would glance at the mirror to make sure that I was smiling. I began to treat my phone conversations as another form of performance. I try to sound as charming as if I were telling a story on the radio.

I soon realized that another vital part of my desk equipment was a list of questions to ask potential bookers when they call. It sounds very professional and puts inexperienced bookers at ease if I take charge by asking key questions that we both need to have answered such as:

- the type of event and kind of stories;
- the date and time of the event and each show;
- the place of the performance and directions for finding it;
- the size, age, seating arrangements, and special requirements of the audience;
- whether there will be an emcee or other introduction; and
- the fee.

Go Get Your Audience

I'm sure many performers have had this experience: you arrive for a show, but your audience doesn't. It happened to me at a toy store in December and at a library in a poor section of town. It is very embarrassing.

Due to lack of funding, staff, and expertise, many institutions fail to advertise their shows or do an absolute minimum. Notices are sent to local papers where they get buried among dozens of other event listings. Poorly designed fliers with little information— sometimes not even your name—are put on counters, in a window, or on a cluttered bulletin board.

The librarian glanced around the empty children's section and said, "Magicians and puppets draw a crowd." It was a slap in the face to me and to storytelling.

The toy store owner was more tactful. "Christmas is a busy season when parents are often more mindful of shopping lists than of children's entertainment," she said. But she did cancel a tentative future booking. Because my other library and children's store shows that year drew crowds of 10 to 200 listeners, I wasn't too concerned. I get the same fee whether my audience is 1 or 1,000 people.

But when I agreed to tell for a bookstore, a coffee shop, and a restaurant the following summer and to be paid either according to how many tickets sold or by tip jar, advertising took on a heightened importance. It meant something to me financially to have a bigger audience. I was already doing a mailing to advertise my newsletter, so it was cost effective to also enclose a flier about my public concerts. Then, during the summer, I brought the flier to my shows at libraries and schools. Many parents and teachers picked them up. I always gave a copy of the flier to the staff person at the site and asked them to post it on a bulletin board. My promotional efforts paid off, and my audiences at the bookstore, coffee shop, and restaurant were sizable. In addition, I got two new bookings from the flier.

I also found that it pays in repeat bookings to have good-sized audiences at my free shows. Librarians have to be concerned about statistics. They generally count the number of people who come to listen. That information is used to convince organizations that sponsor library activities that paying for storytelling is worthwhile because it generates interest in the library.

Help your booker drum up business. It's good public relations. The institutions will appreciate your aid and be more likely to book you again. It will also help put your name out there. The flier you hand to a stranger who has just watched you at a free community festival might wind up in the hands of a club chairperson, a minister looking for workshop leaders, a principal preparing to set up the year's assemblies, or other potential bookers.

It may cost more money to design, print, and mail the flier than you actually make at any one show you advertise, but, believe me, such promotional efforts will pay off down the road.

Resources

Other Versions of "The Vanishing Hitchhiker"

Brunvand, Jan Harold. *The Vanishing Hitchhiker: American Urban Legends and Their Meanings.* New York: W. W. Norton, 1981.

Justice, Jennifer, ed. "The Vanishing Hitchhiker." In *The Ghost & I: Scary Stories for Participatory Telling*, 105–11. Cambridge, MA: Yellow Moon Press, 1992.
The Ghost & I has three sections. One section is for ages five through eight. The second section is for ages nine through eleven. The third section (where the tale "The Vanishing Hitchhiker" is located) is for ages twelve and up.

Leach, Maria. "The Ghostly Hitchhiker." In *The Thing at the Foot of the Bed and Other Scary Tales,* 71–72. Cleveland: World, 1959.

San Souci, Robert, reteller. "Lavender." In *Short & Shivery: Thirty Chilling Tales*, 155–59. New York: Doubleday, 1987.
This collection is best for fourth- and fifth-graders.

Young, Richard, and Judy Dockrey Young. "Last Kiss." In *The Scary Story Reader: Forty-One of the Scariest Stories for Sleepovers, Campfires, Car & Bus Trips—Even for First Dates!*, 34–36. Little Rock, AR: August House, 1993.
This book has stories suitable for middle school students through adults. The Youngs have an afterward in *The Scary Story Reader* that explains the teaching function of gory cautionary tales for adolescents.

Clip Art Publishers

Dover Publications
31 East Second Street
Mineola, NY 11501
Toll free: 800-223-3130
Fax: 212-626-9670

Libraries Unlimited
P.O. Box 6633
Englewood, CO 80155-6633
Toll free: 800-237-6124

Suppliers of Promotional Items

Best Impressions
P.O. Box 802
La Salle, IL 61301
Toll free: 800-635-2378
 Balsa wood gliders, fortune cookie messages, luggage tags, jar openers, pens, wooden nickels, letter openers, stress balloons, rulers, and other items can be imprinted with your name.

The Business Book
P.O. Box 8465
Mankato, MN 56002-8465
Toll free: 800-558-0220
Fax: 507-388-6065
 Caps, shirts, totes, pencils, pens, refrigerator magnets, letter openers, key rings, balloons, rulers, stick-on notes, buttons, mugs, and playing cards can be imprinted with your name.

Oriental Trading Company
P.O. Box 3446
Omaha, NE 68103-3446
Toll free: 800-228-2199
Fax: 800-228-1002
 Balloons, satin ribbons, sunglasses, pompoms, refrigerator magnets, bumper stickers, foam coolers, plastic flyers, sun visors, buttons, megaphones, and pencils can be imprinted with your name. Other give-aways for children include inexpensive toys that can't be imprinted.

Viking Office Products
P.O. Box 61144
Los Angeles, CA 90061-0144
Toll free: 800-421-1222
Fax: 800-762-7329
 Squeeze bottles, pocket mirrors, key rings, paperweights, gift jars, coffee mugs, plastic tumblers, pens, and pencils can be imprinted with your name. Viking has other offices in Washington, Florida, Ohio, Connecticut, and Texas. Call for your closest office.

Further Reading

"A Reader Asks." *The Story Bag: A National Storytelling Newsletter* (December 1994/ January 1995): 4.
 Article about problems a freelance performer has with a local storytelling group.

Huebner, Carol. "Storytelling Goals & Guilds." *The Story Bag: A National Storytelling Newsletter* (February/March 1995): 2–3.
 Response to article in December 1994/ January 1995 issue about a freelance performer who has problems with a local storytelling guild.

Notes

1. Samuel Patrick Smith, "Designing for Dollars," *Laugh Makers: The Variety Arts Magazine for Kidshow and Family Audience Entertainers* 13 (1995): 187–89.

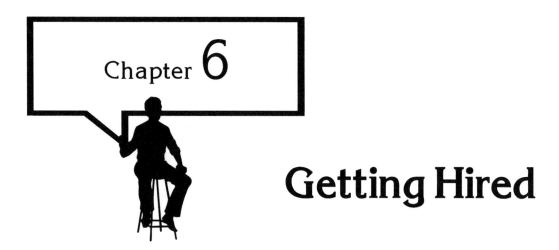

Chapter 6

Getting Hired

All the work that you've done in becoming a polished, professional storyteller means nothing if you have no audience. You must make it easy for potential bookers to find you, and you need to convince them that you are worth their time and money. The work is not over when they call. You still have to close the deal. This involves coming up with reasons for the booker to hire you instead of or in addition to other performers. It's important to sound in charge when first talking with potential bookers, knowing exactly what to ask and how to answer their questions. You must even be professional enough to know when to turn down a job.

Reasons to Hire You

When bookers decide that they want storytelling, they still have to decide which storyteller. Their decision may be based on several factors: cost, ethnic background, experience, and whether they have worked together in the past or are personal friends. You need to know how to make the booker choose YOU.

Uniqueness

What is it that makes you stand out from the crowd of other performers? Are you the only teller who dresses in Renaissance costume and tells tales of that period? Are you the only African American teller in your area? Are you the only storyteller who once taught special education and who therefore understands how to work with special needs students?

Whenever talking to bookers, promote your uniqueness.

Talent and Creativity

While you're not supposed to brag about your own gifts, it's certainly permissible to point out that you are the only local storyteller who's been invited to tell at a folk festival five years in a row, or mention the newspaper article that called you "a bright and shining light in the storytelling world."

Talk about your more creative shows and approaches. You can build your creativity by doing the exercises in Julia Cameron's *The Artist's Way: A Spiritual Path to Higher Creativity*. The exercises can take time and effort, but they can open you up to your true self and let the artist within blossom.

Never denigrate your competition to a potential booker; talk about what you can offer that the other performer can't. Suggest the bookers hire you both! If they decide on the other teller, politely ask that they consider you next year. Then be sure to send them a reminder.

Professionalism

I was once called for a library performance that I felt would be better served by another teller. I recommended the other teller, but the librarian told me that she'd already worked with him and would not do so again. She'd arranged a show for him, and the children came, but the storyteller didn't! The booker called me because she knew she could trust me to not only show up, but to be there early, to have the right sort of tales rehearsed for the occasion, to be dressed appropriately, and to send the invoice and contracts in advance. (See chapter 5 for more advice on presenting yourself professionally.)

Extra Value for the Dollar

Offer little extras to make your services more attractive. Prepare handouts for teachers, use the birthday child's name in a story, create press releases and fliers for the women's club, design a bookmark for the library, or arrange radio interviews to promote a folk festival. If your clients book you for three shows, consider lowering your fee, throwing in an extra show, or paying some of your own expenses.

When I was hired by the Children's Museum to tell in shows for three different months, I informed the program director that I had taken out three ads in a local family magazine listing the museum programs as well as my other shows. I also passed out fliers listing the upcoming performances at my other shows. This was free advertising for the museum. I suggested that she ask companies that market food to children to be corporate sponsors for her storytelling series as they might also provide free food samples, such as

cookies or fruit snacks, for the kids. The director was thrilled with the added value I was giving her and the museum.

Audiences like extras too. The summer that I told dog stories at the public libraries, I told the children that if they were good listeners, they would leave with a new dog. At the end of my show, I handed out large squares of white paper and taught the children how to make origami dog faces. The librarians appreciated my suggesting that the kids read origami books to get more ideas.

The chieftain of a Highland festival was approached by two storytellers with Scottish backgrounds: another performer and me. One reason he hired me was that I have my own portable, battery-operated sound system, saving him the expense of renting a system. The system, which fits the mike, stand, speaker, and sound box all in a briefcase, cost me $500 in 1991. It was recommended to me by Mark Wade, an experienced ventriloquist. Many storytellers have their own microphones that they bring so that the sound is better. Promote this as extra value and as a sign of your professionalism.

Give-Away Ideas

When you are taking bookings for parties or holiday shows, offer to bring a "gift" or party favor for each person. It might make the difference between whether you are booked or not. Be sure to figure in the cost of the materials and your time when calculating your fee.

When I am handing out origami figures at a children's party, I always fold one at the end of my performance to demonstrate how it's done. Then I have each child close his or her eyes and reach into a bag to pull out one of the already folded figures to take home. Because children are sticklers for fairness, I make all the figures the same—only the colors are different. I always fold more figures than are needed so that I can give the extras to adults and babies.

You can find many books on origami at the public library. If you'd like to combine paper folding and storytelling, see Nancy Schimmel's book, *Just Enough to Make a Story: A Sourcebook for Storytellers.*

Another idea, also suitable for either children or adults, is to write a story or poem for the holidays or for a birthday celebration and print it on pretty paper. Roll each copy into a tube and tie with a piece of ribbon or yarn. (This makes it look much nicer than handing out a flat sheet of paper.) Include your name, address, and phone number at the bottom of the handout.

Other items you can distribute as freebies include customized stick-on labels or refrigerator magnets. These giveaways can be handed out from a pretty basket. Remember, presentation is important! See the "Resources" section of chapter 5 for the names and addresses of companies that sell these items.

Recommendations

Whenever possible, tell potential bookers about people they know and respect who recommend your services. If an Episcopalian pastor calls about a workshop for Sunday School teachers, quote the praise you earned from another pastor of his denomination. If the local PTA president calls, suggest that she call the principal of a nearby school for a recommendation of your assemblies.

Whenever you perform, distribute several business cards and brochures and ask bookers to tell others about you. A minister may have a monthly breakfast with other ministers at which she could pass out your card. A mother could tell others in her parenting class how wonderful you were with the kids at her child's birthday party.

Questions You Should Be Ready to Answer Before the Booker Hires You

Potential bookers have the right to certain information about your experience, your programs, and your expectations regarding fees, telling conditions, and so on. The following are some of the questions you should be prepared to answer:

- What experience do you have telling to my particular age group or situation?

- How many years have you been telling?

- Can you provide references from other bookers in my area or elsewhere?

- What do you charge? (Answer this question only after they have explained for exactly what service they are hiring you.)

- Can you send me a brochure or other information?

- Where can I hear you tell? (Most bookers won't mind outside observers at your show, but get their permission, anyway.)

- Do you have a tape, CD, or videotape of stories I could view? (Create an audition tape of a short performance, and distribute it with copies of your brochure or fliers. Make sure the tape contains all of the information necessary to contact you. Some tellers have found that their audition tapes were copied and distributed to several potential bookers. If you wish to have your tape returned, enclose a self-addressed, stamped envelope in your mailing. It's better to leave it with the booker and suggest the tape be shared with other potential bookers.

Questions You Should Ask

When potential bookers call you for information, find out their name, position, and the organization they represent. Ask if they are looking for a storyteller for a specific occasion, date, or age level. It may save time for you both if you have a prior commitment on that date or don't have material suitable to the event. You may wish to suggest someone who can fulfill the requirements—make sure you know who you are recommending and can stand behind the quality of their performances—and how to get in touch with them. Chapter 5 covers in more depth how to talk to bookers. Chapter 7 discusses specific questions to ask school chairpeople.

Know Your Competition

Attend shows by other variety artists and storytellers in your market. If their shows are open to the public, this will be easy to do. If the show is a private event, ask for the performer's permission and that of the booker.

When you observe a colleague, ask yourself the following questions:

- How is this performer different from you? How are you alike?

- Does the performer do a better job of "working the crowd" or making transitions between stories?

- Does the performer have skills you don't, such as playing a musical instrument or singing?

- Is the performer telling the same stories you tell? Does he or she tell the same stories but in a different way?

- Is the performer charging more or less than you?

- How does the performer advertise?

- Why do you think the same bookers should hire you the next time?

Try not to get discouraged if you watch another performer put on a flawless show. If you can't think of a single reason why you should be hired over another person, find someone who can give you a pep talk about how wonderful you are; reread letters of thanks and glowing newspaper articles; and remember the rapt faces of past audiences. This will help you remember that you are just as valuable as the nationally known tellers.

Competitors, Colleagues, and Friends

The storytelling world is a small, intimate one. There are very few tellers who keep themselves apart from others in their field. So while you may have to compete with your friends and colleagues for some jobs, it's important to cultivate respect and good will.

If someone calls me for a gig I can't make, I recommend other tellers who might be more available or suitable and give the booker their phone numbers. I always ask the caller to tell the other performer of my recommendation. I hope my colleague will return the favor and recommend me in the future.

If you are going to be presenting in a new area, try to find a friend or colleague from that area to help you arrange other bookings and give you advice on what local bookers pay (though many schools are willing to pay out-of-town performers more than local tellers). Such cooperative arrangements can be beneficial for both tellers. If you are successful in the new location, it will promote storytelling in the region, possibly leading to more bookings for your colleague. You can also reciprocate and assist colleagues who come to tell in your "territory."

How Can Bookers Hire You If They Can't Find You?

In chapter 4, I discussed getting your name, address, and phone number out to potential bookers and audiences, but I can't emphasize enough the importance of getting known by these people and of making it easy for them to find you. When people in your area think "entertainer" or "storyteller," they should think of you. When they want to call you, your phone number should be readily available on business cards, mailings, advertisements, and in phone books. Once a woman actually checked property records at the county office to track me down. All she had to do was look in the telephone book under my name!

Turning Down Bookings

Sometimes you or your booker—whether a corporation, festival, club, or individuals—is disappointed in your show. Maybe the event would have been better suited to a clown, juggler, mime, singer, or other form of entertainment. While it's hard to give up a possible gig, a reputable performer will sometimes ask, "Are you sure you want to hire a storyteller for this particular event?"

For example, I was once asked to perform at a company picnic. The bookers planned live bands and games all day long. It was going to be held outside in a spot with no shade, and the only seating would be in the food court. It was clearly not turning into a good setup for storytelling. I explained to the booker that storytelling requires a quiet environment where people are not squinting in the sun, sitting on dirt, too hot to focus, and listening with one ear to other noises. I suggested that a walk-around act such as a clown might be a better idea, but asked that they keep me in mind for other gatherings.

A talent agency asked whether I could enact a murder mystery for the spouses at a conference. I have no murder mysteries in my repertoire and had no time to research, learn, and rehearse one before the banquet. So reluctantly I had to say no.

In the end, the good will you can get from not taking inappropriate jobs can lead to better jobs that you will be happy to be remembered for.

Sell Now for Later

Even when giving one show, think about how to sell your next program to the audience. After presenting Christmas stories at the preschool, talk to the principal about your Easter show. If a college professor enjoyed your lecture on American folktales, suggest a lecture on European folklore. The librarian who saw how much the parents enjoyed participating in the stories with their children may be interested in a parent workshop. After the birthday party, be sure to mention that you also perform at Hanukkah gatherings.

At every booking, hand out business cards and pass out fliers about your products. Follow up with mailings and phone calls, but the time to sell for later is now, while your bookers are still enthusiastic about what you've done. If they seem interested, try to get a commitment. Offer incentives, such as, "If you put down $10 now on the next workshop, you'll get a 10 percent discount on the total fee." Ask if there are any questions. Walk that tightrope between being considered pushy and giving potential bookers something they genuinely want.

Resources

Further Reading

Cameron, Julia. *The Artist's Way: A Spiritual Path to Higher Creativity.* New York: Putnam, 1992.

Schimmel, Nancy. *Just Enough to Make a Story: A Sourcebook for Storytellers.* Berkeley, CA: Sisters' Choice Books and Recordings, 1992.

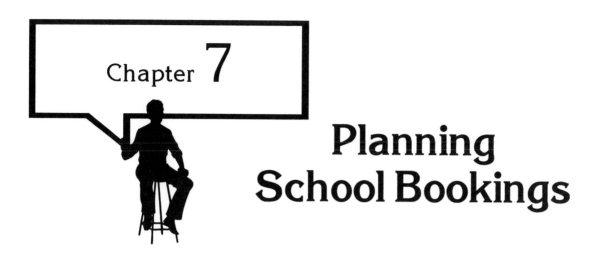

Chapter 7

Planning School Bookings

Nationally known storyteller and author Heather Forest, who has hundreds of bookings to keep in order, has developed her own planning procedure. She has a notebook with three sections: Inquiry, Hold, and Engagement. When a booker calls to find out more about her, she fills out her booking sheet and puts it in the Inquiry section. When they call back or during the original phone conversation ask her to hold a particular date while they make their final decision, then she moves the sheet to the Hold section. When they finally make a firm commitment to hire her, she moves the sheet to the Engagement section. Each section is in order by date.

Reread chapter 4 if you need ideas on how to sell schools on the educational value of storytelling. Once you've convinced schools to book you, this chapter will help you prepare for a new school year.

What to Do First

Start preparing for your school shows during the summer. Decide whether to work only with elementary school students or if you're willing to create shows suitable for adolescents and to go into middle schools and high schools. Choose which school districts you are going to target and decide how far you are willing to travel. Decide if you want to work up new shows to publicize this year. Create or update your handouts of storytelling activities and bibliographies of suggested books and tapes.

Create School Packets Ahead of Time

Estimate how many schools will hire you during the year. Using manila envelopes, assemble packets for each school, filling each with:

- booking sheet (see "When You Get a Call," p. 60) that lists the questions you ask bookers about specific events

- #10 stamped business envelope with your return address

- #9 stamped, self-addressed envelope, which will fit into the #10 envelope

- cover letter

- "Preparing Students for a Storytelling Experience" handout (see chapter 3 for my version of this handout. You will want to develop your own.)

- blank index card or page for a loose-leaf notebook

- sheet of paper with the word *Calendar* written or typed on it

- two copies of a blank contract

- teacher handouts and cover letter in a portfolio with pockets

You will be using these items in specific ways as your performance dates get closer. Some tellers prefer to create their packets as each booking comes in.

Make Contacts

Send letters to the assembly chairpersons (usually a PTA member or the principal or another staff member) in charge of booking events at the schools you want to visit. Some schools have a PTO or Parent/Teacher Group instead of the PTA. Some schools start booking as early as May for the following school year. Others won't call you until a week before they want you for an assembly. I generally do my mailings in September. Some performers do both a spring and a fall mailing.

Explain your offerings and fees in your mailing and include a promotional brochure. Ask the event coordinator to share the information with the principal. Follow up by phone to make sure that the mailing was received by the appropriate person. You may have to leave a message.

When You Get a Call

When a principal, librarian, or PTA chairperson calls for a booking, speak professionally and with a smile in your voice. Ask the booker the following questions, which should be included on a "booking sheet," a customized form on which you record all information about each performance you arrange:

1. When do you want the performance?

   Check your schedule or calendar. Record the assembly times and the name of the school next to the date and on the booking sheet clipped to the school packet. I like to carry an appointment book with me at all times so I can tell interested people where my next public show is or set up future engagements while I'm face to face with the person.

2. When will the shows begin and end?

   When scheduling, allow at least 15 minutes between each assembly for getting groups in and out and for late starts. Tell the booker if you are willing to vary the length of your shows according to the requirements of the school. For example, they might prefer a 20-minute assembly for the kindergartners and a 40-minute assembly for the sixth-graders. If you are to be at the school for the entire day, request breaks for rest and lunch.

3. What grade levels will attend each show?

   Recommend that younger students and older students not be included in the same audience. If that's unavoidable, prepare stories appropriate to both kindergartners and sixth-graders.

   My favorite way of breaking grade levels up is to put kindergartners through second-graders in one assembly, third- and fourth-graders in another assembly, and fifth- and sixth-graders in a third assembly. In districts where sixth-graders are put into middle schools with the seventh- and eighth-graders, I group the third- through fifth-graders together.

4. What type of stories do you want told?

    The publicity you've already sent to the school should have listed the names of your shows and given a brief synopsis of what is covered in each.

5. What type of stories should I not tell?

    Sometimes there are types of stories that should be avoided. At one school, a student's mother had been killed in a car accident two days before my show. If someone had not warned me of this, I would have told a ghost story in which a mother died.

    If a school asks me not to tell a certain kind of story, I will oblige, but I do prefer to know of these requests in advance, not five minutes before my first assembly. I will sometimes delicately broach the topic if it's not brought up. Once when I was asked to tell at a small rural school, I was warned not to tell any tales with supernatural themes. Two years later when I was invited back, the parent who arranged my visit didn't mention this taboo. I had made a note of it during my first visit, so I asked. It turned out the parent was new to the community and unaware of the requirement, but the principal confirmed that some parents would be offended by supernatural themes. (While I told no spooky stories there, a few parents still complained about the violence in my traditional folktales.)

6. Are there special populations I should target?

    If you know that your audience will contain non-native speakers of English, offer to tell bilingual stories if you know any. You can tell stories from the native cultures of the students.

    If your audience will include hearing-impaired students, find out if the school prefers that their students read lips or if you should use sign language while telling your story. If the student will have a translator sign the stories to them, give the translator copies or verbal summaries of your stories. One translator with whom

I worked had never heard of tempura, which was an important part of a story I was telling. I explained the term to her in advance, so she could sign its meaning to the students.

7. How do I get to the school?

    Write the directions down and include the school's address and phone number. Keep the directions on file, so when you're asked to return, you won't have to ask for directions again. Inform your booker that you will arrive at least 30 minutes before your first show.

8. Where should I send my contract and invoice?

    Find out who should receive the contract and where to send it. Tell the booker you will send two copies of your contract. Ask that he or she check the form for accuracy and that one copy be signed and returned to you in the stamped, self-addressed #9 envelope enclosed.

    Be sure to clearly state your fee and whether you require an advance deposit. I generally soften the blow by adding, "For that price you also receive a packet of handouts to copy for the teachers so that they can follow up my visit with creative writing exercises in the classroom." Find out when and in what form the school needs your invoice. The school may send you a special form to fill out.

9. What are the school's and the booker's phone numbers?

    Having the event coordinator's home phone number may come in handy if you need to call after school hours because of an emergency or a pressing question.

10. Can your school provide me with . . . ?

    This is your chance to relate your specific needs and requirements, such as having the children seated in rows on the floor, a mike on a stand, a glass of water, a blackboard, a videocassette player, a particular type of introduction, and so on.

If you will be at the school through the lunch hour, request that lunch be provided. If you need accommodations for the night, other meals, expenses covered, transportation, and so on, explain these requirements to the booker.

In addition to these questions, your booking sheet can contain a "to-do" checklist of tasks you need to accomplish before the show:

send the contract, photos, a biography, a fee schedule, and references; bring a map, the sound system, handouts, your name sign, a bell for calling the audience to attention, and other necessities; send a thank-you note after the performance. The booking sheet can also include a section for remarks about the conversation or notes about the performance to reference in the event of another show with that booker.

Get Ready

After your phone conversation with the booker in which you've learned the answers to all of the above questions, type the details into your contract, using a carbon (or computer) to make two copies. Send the contract to the booker along with the SASE and your invoice, if needed. Your contract should include the following information:

- booker's name and phone number
- school name, address, and phone number
- directions to the school
- performance date
- times of shows
- grade levels to be in each show
- fee and payment conditions
- performance instructions

If the show is to take place within six weeks, also send a "Before the Storyteller's Visit" handout. If the show is scheduled for later in the year, put the handout in another envelope addressed to the booker, and mail it a few weeks before your visit.

Type the name of the school, the date of your performance, and your agreed-upon fee on the blank index card in your school packet. On the day of your performance, jot down the stories you told. This way, you won't duplicate the program if you return the next year. While some students love hearing stories repeated, others may become bored enough to disrupt. Plan new shows for the school by looking at your notes about previous shows.

On the paper headed "Calendar," enter the date of your performance, the school, and the fee. When you perform, note on this form whether you have been paid or will have to wait for your check. Put this on a master accounting calendar. When you receive payment, note this on the calendar. Check periodically to keep track of past-due accounts. If you haven't received payment after six weeks, call the school district's accounting department or PTA treasurer. This is important. A fellow storyteller who only haphazardly makes note of whether he has received payment told me of a phone call he received from a teacher who informed him that he hadn't yet been paid for a student workshop he'd given two months before. It's a good thing the teacher noticed, because the storyteller hadn't!

Don't Forget the Packet

I keep the manila envelopes for my bookings in chronological order in my office. The day before a performance, I pull out the envelope and make sure it contains the packet and any other items I need to take. I make final decisions about what stories I will be telling and rehearse my tales yet again. I gather together items such as my workshop flip chart, maps of the area, my sign, and my portable sound system. I assemble all of these items and place them by the door so I can grab them when I am ready to leave in the morning. I pick out my dress and jewelry for the event and hang them up at the front of my closet.

With all this preparation, I'm not frantically trying to remember where I put my workshop handouts or find a pair of earrings that match my costume five minutes before I have to leave. I leave with plenty of time to get to the school, check in at the office, and set up my assembly space. I'm ready, and I'm as stress-free and professional as I can be.

Resources

Further Reading

Blatt, Gloria. *Once upon a Folktale: Capturing the Folklore Process with Children.* New York: Teachers College Press, 1993.

Bosma, Bette. *Fairy Tales, Fables, Legends, and Myths: Using Folk Literature in Your Classroom.* New York: Teachers College Press, 1992.

Clarkson, Atelia, and Gilbert Cross. *World Folktales: A Scribner Resource Collection.* New York: Charles Scribner's Sons, 1980.
Read introductions to each chapter and the section "Folktales in the Elementary Classroom."

Coles, Robert. *The Call of Stories: Teaching and the Moral Imagination.* Boston: Houghton Mifflin, 1989.

Davis, Donald. *The Story Creating Handbook: A Resource for Family Storytelling, Classroom Story Creation, and Personal Journaling.* Little Rock, AR: August House, 1993.

Denman, Gregory. *Sit Tight, and I'll Swing You a Tail . . . : Using and Writing Stories with Young People.* Portsmouth, NH: Heinemann, 1991.

Dieckmann, Jim. "From That Day to This: Storytelling in Environmental Education." *The Story Bag Newsletter* (January 1989): 2–4.

Dubrovin, Vivian. *Create Your Own Storytelling Stories.* Masonville, CO: Storycraft, 1995.

Farrell, Catharine. *Storytelling: A Guide for Teachers.* New York: Scholastic Professional Books, 1991.

Geisler, Harlynne. *Storytelling in the Schools.* San Diego, 1994.
This packet of handouts includes 29 curriculum activities, 11 inspirations for creative writing, and 12 bibliographies listing everything from storytelling techniques to books on folk superstitions. Send $5.50 to cover the cost of photocopying and mailing to *Story Bag: A National Storytelling Newsletter*, 5361 Javier Street, San Diego, CA 92117-3215, 619-569-9399.

Gillard, Marni. *Storyteller, Storyteacher: Discovering the Power of Storytelling for Teaching and Living.* York, ME: Stenhouse, 1996.

Griffin, Barbara Budge. *Storyteller's Journal: A Guidebook for Story Research and Learning.* Medford, OR, 1990.
For order information on Barbara Budge Griffin's books, contact her at: Storyteller Guide Book, P.O. Box 626, Medford, OR 97501, 503-773-3006.

———. *Storyteller's Workbook.* Medford, OR: Storyteller Guide Book, 1990.

———. *Student Storyfest: How to Organize a Storytelling Festival.* Medford, OR: Storyteller Guide Book, 1989.

———. *Students as Storytellers: The Long and the Short of Learning a Story.* Medford, OR: Storyteller Guide Book, 1989.

Heflick, David. *How to Make Money Performing in the Public Schools*. Orient, WA: Silcox Productions, 1993.

Practical information from a musician's point of view. Write Silcox Productions, P.O. Box 1407, Orient, WA 99160.

Jenkins, Peggy. *The Joyful Child: A Sourcebook of Activities and Ideas for Releasing Children's Natural Joy*. Tucson, AZ: Harbinger House, 1989.

Livo, Norma J., and Sandra A. Reitz. *Storytelling Activities*. Englewood, CO: Libraries Unlimited, 1987.

Maguire, Jack. *Creative Storytelling: Choosing, Inventing, and Sharing Tales with Children*. New York: McGraw-Hill, 1985.

Paley, Vivian Gussin. *The Boy Who Would Be a Helicopter: The Uses of Storytelling in the Classroom*. Cambridge, MA: Harvard University Press, 1990.

Pellowski, Anne. *The Storytelling Handbook: A Young People's Collection of Unusual Tales and Helpful Hints on How to Tell Them*. New York: Simon & Schuster Books for Young Readers, 1995.

Schutz-Gruber, Barbara. *Trickster Tales from Around the World: An Interdisciplinary Guide for Teachers*. Ann Arbor, MI, 1991.

An audiocassette is also available from Barbara Schutz-Gruber, 2855 Kimberly, Ann Arbor, MI 48104, 313-761-5118.

Visual and Performing Arts Framework for California Public Schools: Kindergarten Through Grade Twelve. Curriculum Frameworks and Instructional Materials Section, California State Department of Education, 1982.

Lists goals for students, developmental level charts, program development, evaluation of student progress, and more. Can be ordered from the department by writing P.O. Box 271, Sacramento, CA 95802. See if your state's Department of Education has a similar framework on which you can develop and organize your curriculum handouts.

Wason-Ellam, Linda. *Start with a Story: Literature and Learning in Your Classroom*. Portsmouth, NH: Heinemann, 1991.

Witherell, Carol, and Nel Noddings, eds. *Stories Lives Tell: Narrative and Dialogue in Education*. New York: Teachers College Press, 1991.

Chapter 8

Special Projects
Workshops, Concerts, and Tapes

Sometimes you will want extra money and exposure. Other times, you may have a topic you are interested in exploring in a workshop, tape, or concert, but no one is interested in hiring you to do it. Perhaps the only way that this special project is going to happen is if you invest in it yourself.

Workshops and Classes

I differentiate between workshops, lectures, and classes in this way: Workshops actively engage the participants during at least part of the time. Lectures are primarily speeches with some stories and question-and-answer sessions. Classes involve more than one meeting and are often sponsored by an educational institution. These are my working definitions, and they are not set in cement.

Chapter 1 lists some of the places where you may give workshops, lectures, and classes. What I'd like to address here is sponsoring a workshop or class yourself. The steps involved in planning and conducting the event are the same no matter who sponsors it. The difference here is that you have more freedom in every aspect of the workshop, from selecting the topic to deciding the time involved. You are only limited by what you think your participants will be willing to pay to learn. Of course, all the initial expense and advertising of the event are now on your shoulders.

Picking a Topic

Where is your strongest area of expertise? It may not be straight storytelling. Perhaps you want to combine information about storytelling with your interest or experience in other areas. I combined three interests in a university class called "Creative Dramatics, Puppetry, and Storytelling." My internal debates about how I can call myself a feminist and still tell traditional fairy tales led to the lecture, "Is Cinderella Dead?" that I gave during Women's Opportunity Week. My fascination with Jungian psychology caused me to join the Friends of Jung and give a workshop titled "An Encounter with Folk Tales and Myths."

Here are the titles of 30 other workshops, lectures, and classes that I have given. They may spark some ideas of your own.

- Bookmagic: Children's Literature for Teachers and Parents
- Climbing the Three Steps: Finding, Learning, and Telling a Story
- Creating Improvisational Stories for Children and Adults
- Creating Stories with an Audience
- Creative Writing Games
- Exploring Stories from Other Cultures
- Fighting the Giants in Your Life
- Folktale Roots in Europe
- From Storytelling to Creative Writing
- Gestures and Words
- Get Kids Involved: Participation Stories for Children
- Getting Started in Storytelling
- Got a Minute? Short, Short Folk Tales
- The Hero and Heroine in Storytelling
- The How and Why of Porquoi Folk Tales
- How to Plan, Prepare, and Put on a Problem-Free Preschool Program (conducted jointly with Martha Holloway)
- The Inner Magic of Fairy Tales: The Traditional and the Unexplored
- Magic, Miracles and Mystery: A Journey in Storytelling
- Oral Communication
- Religious Storytelling
- See! Hear! Do! 11 Methods of Learning a Story to Tell
- Select, Learn and Tell: The Basics of Storytelling
- Stories and String Figures
- Storytelling in the Classroom
- Storytelling: Words and Music
- Storytelling: You Can Too!
- Storytelling's Link with Creative Writing
- Tell a Tale: Telling Stories in the Classroom
- Traditional Storytelling For All Ages
- Urban Legends

Recycle

I was once asked to give a three-hour lecture on ghost stories at the University of San Diego. I titled it "Delicious Shivers: Tales of the Supernatural." I have since used the hard work I put into developing the lecture to develop one- and two-hour workshops at a local reading association conference, a state library association conference, a library class for San Jose State University, the local clown club, a Storytelling Institute at the International Reading Association Conference, the International Whole Language Umbrella Conference, the Illini Storytellers Guild, a folk festival, and two self-sponsored workshops. Sometimes I changed the name to "Delicious Shivers: Spooky Stories" if I thought the participants might only be working with children and might be put off by the word *supernatural*.

Gathering Information

Jot down what you know about the topic you have chosen. Gather together any notes you have from previous classes on similar topics, books and tapes on the subject, and bibliographies. If you need further information, get in touch with experts in the field or do more research.

Organize the information. It's a good idea to intersperse stories, breaks, and participation activities throughout the workshop so that the interest level stays high.

Time your workshop. Remember that participants' questions can eat up a lot of time. Decide whether you want to answer questions as they come up or have participants save them until the end of the workshop. Consider taking question-and-answer breaks periodically.

Maybe you have so much information that you want to organize a class that will meet several times rather than a workshop. This involves a bigger time commitment from you and from your participants.

Location

I have used three different sites over the years to put on workshops: a meeting room in a bank, a social hall in a church, and my own living room. When I have 10 or fewer participants, I like my home best. It's most convenient for me, and even forces me to thoroughly clean my house each time! Plus it's free—although the bank allowed me to use their room at no charge as long as I had a minimum balance in a savings account and my in-laws' small church also let me use their hall free. I told the church members that they could attend any of my workshops free if they registered with me in advance, and one member did come to one workshop. You may hesitate to make a similar offer of free registration if you're using a hall at a large church or temple where dozens of members might wish to come.

Publicizing Your Workshop

Chapter 5 covers how to publicize your event through direct mailings, fliers, press releases, and ads. I take fliers about my workshops to every school I visit for the six to eight weeks prior to the workshop and ask that they be placed in staff mailboxes or put in the faculty lounge. I tell my friends to tell their friends. I enclose a copy of the flier with all my correspondence. I hand out fliers wherever I go within 120 miles of the workshop location. I have had people travel that far to attend my workshops.

If I am putting on the workshop at my own expense, I do not list the exact location. Participants must register in advance and pay in full before I send them directions. This accomplishes two things. It gives me an exact count of participants, so I can prepare workshop packets with handouts, resource information, and other materials without going to the expense of making up extras. It also forces the participants to make a firm commitment because, as it states on my flier, refunds minus a $5 processing fee are only given with a 24-hour notice of cancellation.

Preparing Participants for a Workshop

I always tell the participants exactly how I want them to prepare for the workshop and what materials they need to bring—from crayons to stories to comfortable clothes. This information can be included on the flier or passed on by phone or letter after participants sign up for the event.

Beginning the Workshop

It seems that someone is always late. Compensate for this fact when determining your schedule so you will not lose several minutes waiting for tardy participants or catching each one up as he or she arrives. Another way to handle late arrivals is to begin by asking people to fill out a short questionnaire as they arrive, answering questions such as:

- What is your present job? [*Knowing that you have a minister in your audience of mostly librarians and teachers might prompt you to occasionally refer to religious stories as well as stories suitable for schools and libraries.*]

- What ages do you wish to tell to? [*If you are giving a basic storytelling workshop, it's a good idea to know if everyone only plans to tell to preschoolers and primary students or if you have a high school teacher and an aspiring adult performer mixed into the pack.*]

- Why are you taking this workshop? [*The participants' aspirations may surprise you. Maybe you thought they were all nurses who wished to tell stories to cancer patients, but one of them writes down that she intends to become a freelance storyteller and wants to know all the steps involved. Knowing this, you can speak to her during the break about other workshops you are giving on the topic, books she could read, and your willingness to be a mentor for free or for compensation.*]

- What is one question you'd like answered about storytelling? [*These questions can help you make last-minute changes. For example, if several people want to know about technique, you may plan to spend more than the 15 minutes you'd originally allotted to the topic.*]

Collect the questionnaires as people finish them. When the official beginning time of your workshop arrives, give the participants an activity to complete. Have the directions for the activity written on a blackboard or included in the participants' packets so that you don't have to repeat the instructions for latecomers. While the activity is going on, read the questionnaires and plan to answer them at a specific time or throughout the workshop.

Extras

I always provide some refreshments at my workshops (e.g., bottled water, tea, coffee, and homemade muffins), and my participants really seem to appreciate it. It doesn't have to cost much, and every penny is paid back in good will.

If I have free posters from educational conferences or leftover catalogs or advertising fliers, I give them away at my workshops. Sometimes I give them to the first people to show up in appreciation for their being timely. Sometimes I give them as a thanks to participants who helped during the workshop. I may even request additional catalogs from companies with materials that fit the theme of my workshop.

If you have created storytelling tapes or books, you can sell them at the workshop or include the cost in your workshop fee and give them to participants as a bonus.

Ending the Workshop

End with a story. Thank the participants, and tell them of your upcoming events and availability as a performer. Give them one last chance to buy your tapes and books and hand out an evaluation form.

Concerts

Although dictionaries usually define a "concert" as a musical performance, the term is used in the storytelling world to refer to a show. A storytelling concert can be a private or public performance of one or more tellers at any time of day or evening for any age audience. There is no set length of time that a concert lasts. It can have a particular focus—such as family stories, ghostly tales, or narratives of a particular author—but even that is not necessary. It may be held in any locale, indoors or out.

Every experienced teller has been part of a concert of several performers and has also put on one-person shows.

Refer back to chapter 2 for suggestions on organizing your shows into themes, choosing a time of year to hold a show, choosing an audience to target, picking costumes, adding participation, and creating beginnings and endings to your shows. *Doing It Right in L.A.: Self-Producing for the Performing Artist* by Jacki Apple provides in-depth advice on producing a concert, whether or not you live in Los Angeles.

Emceeing a Storytelling Concert

When a concert includes several tellers, an emcee plays an important role in weaving the different stories, styles, and performers into a coherent event. There is an art to being a good emcee, which is why you will notice that some people appear as emcees on so many different programs across the nation. They are asked to perform their magical act of emceeing again and again, because they've proven their ability.

After several poor introductions (and, believe me, it will happen to you over and over again in the course of your career), you will begin to appreciate the talented emcee who can build anticipation in your audience, making them want to hear your tales.

The Introduction

Prior to the concert, ask the participating tellers if they want to write their own introductions. If not, ask if there's anything special they want mentioned, such as work they've done or the title of a story. Review what you know about each performer, and try to personalize the introduction. Consider, for example, mentioning the first time you heard the teller and what impressed you most about the person's stories or character.

Storytelling Trivia

If your audience is new to storytelling, include some interesting facts about the tradition in your introduction. Also, if the locale has a storytelling group or festival, include this information and urge the audience to attend a meeting or concert.

Order of Storytellers

The performance order depends on the tellers involved. Some prefer to go first, others prefer to go last. Other considerations include balancing the program, following a sad story with a funny one, scheduling a scary story before a funny one so the audience won't laugh inappropriately, and so on. Try to schedule long tales early or intersperse them with short ones. Put a long story before the break, so the audience has a chance to digest it and relax before hearing more tales. Always begin and end the program with strong performers. This warms up the audience and leaves them with a pleasant memory of the event.

Time Limitations

A good emcee has to be ruthless about time limits—though in a polite way. Explain several days or weeks ahead of time that each tale must be so many minutes long and no longer. Warn the performers that the program must be kept to a reasonable length and that tellers who go over the allotted time will be cut off by the emcee. Tell them a signal will be given when one minute is left and another signal when time has run out. Position yourself or a timekeeper so the performer can see the signals: one finger for one minute and the finger moving across the throat for "finish up now." If the performer ignores the final signal, come on stage and say, "I know you'll all want to ask how that story ends after the concert. Our next teller is. . . ."

Special Requirements

If the storytellers need to prepare stories to meet a certain theme, tell them long in advance. I performed at a concert where the emcee casually mentioned in her introduction that the theme that night was tales of love. I was taken entirely unawares and had to fumble through my own introduction to the tale, trying to make a rather lame connection to the theme. The next teller had the same problem: he hadn't been told either.

I've also been booked into places where I was handed a wireless microphone with a battery pack attached but had no pocket to tuck it into or belt to attach it to, so I had to hold the battery pack during my show. Let your tellers know the sound and microphone arrangements in advance so they can plan their clothing accordingly.

Try to accommodate performer requests if at all possible. I once gave an emcee a two-sentence introduction I'd written and asked him to read it. He looked at it, said he never read introductions, got up on the stage, and meandered through a boring description of me that didn't at all set the atmosphere I wished to create. In most situations where it seems likely that the person who booked me will massacre my name, woodenly read a written introduction, fumble through a sentence or two while continually asking me if what is said is correct, make me sound much more wonderful than I can possibly live up to, or give me back-handed compliments, I forestall this agony by insisting I introduce myself.

The Big Night

Ask performers to arrive at least 30 to 60 minutes early. Test the volume levels on the sound system and make sure the items requested by the tellers—chairs, water, and so forth—are on the stage or ready to be carried on. Show the tellers where they should wait before going on stage.

Briefly welcome the audience to the concert. Keep those pesky "housekeeping" remarks about future concerts or where the bathrooms are to a minimum. Set the mood for the evening. At the end of the concert, finish with brief closing remarks or possibly a song.

Although the organizers of the concert may handle many of the details mentioned here, don't assume anything. As emcee, find out about your shared responsibilities.

Tapes

Hundreds of experienced storytellers have recorded audiocassettes, generally at their own expense. Several have recorded videotapes for commercial companies or made short audition videotapes that are not intended for sale. One or two have even made compact discs. These recordings serve many purposes:

- They can be used as auditions.

- They serve as a record of where a teller was artistically at a particular period in her or his career.

- They are excellent ways to explore different art forms.

- They can provide another source of income (and outgo, as the initial expense can be high).

- They answer audience demand for a way to take storytellers home.

- They are proof that a freelance teller is no longer a beginner—unless the tape itself is painfully amateurish.

Determine your reasons for making a tape. Decide who your intended audience will be: librarians, teachers, therapists, preschoolers, adolescents, seniors, and so on. The audience might be a combination of different groups, but it is a rare tape that is all things to all listeners. A tape of bedtime stories for preschoolers will have a different sound than a tape of healing tales for cancer patients.

Make sure you have permission to use any stories owned by someone else. Find experts who respect your artistic vision: engineers, directors, and artists to design the J-card (the paper insert on which the title and notes of the cassette are printed) and flier. Listen to or view the tapes of other storytellers (see the "Resources" section for ordering information) to get ideas. Research the costs, and budget your money. Rehearse, rehearse, rehearse. Record these rehearsals, and listen to them. Refine your stories. Time them so that they fit on the length of tape you've chosen. Be prepared when you enter the studio.

Creating an Audiotape or Videocassette: The Voices of Experience

The following advice comes from the participants in a 1995 storytelling retreat, who agreed to discuss what they have learned from making, researching, marketing, and listening to tapes. The retreat members included Barbara Budge Griffin, Angela Lloyd, Olga Loya, Sandra MacLees, and Kathleen Zundell.

Find an engineer who's worked with the spoken word, not just music. Ask for demos of his or her work to listen to. Do a test run with the engineer. Have your voice recorded as you go high and low in sound and tone. Listen to the test. Is there any feedback? Also be sure to record words with "esses" and "pees" so you can hear if they pop or sound sibilant.

When planning your stories, be aware if there are parts that are visual. Is the meaning conveyed by facial expression or gesture or body stance? If so, you are going to have to translate those meanings into words and vocal expression that someone listening to your tape will understand. It's not just recording your performance; it's a whole new creation. Hone your stories and put color in your voice. Rehearse, rehearse, rehearse.

Music and sound effects can really enhance stories. If you use musicians, work with them before you go into the studio so that expensive studio time won't be wasted while you show them how to play. Olga has music start and end each side of her tape. The music continues to play as she starts to tell, and then fades away softly. It's very effective.

Find a director whom you trust and who has experience working on storytelling tapes. Kathleen Zundell used Carol Birch, who is wonderful, but Kathleen didn't always follow her advice. She decided that children answering questions and participating in her stories would sound great on her tape despite Carol's advice to the contrary. Kathleen is glad that she trusted herself because she still enjoys listening to those sections on the cassette.

Some directors recommend that you script your stories, writing them out.

Sandra remembered, "I couldn't create a script, but I find rehearsing my stories and timing them works just as well."

When recording, close your eyes and imagine telling the stories to one person rather than to a large audience. It made the telling sound intimate. Olga did it differently. She found a friend with a very responsive face who wanted to come to the studio. She told directly to her. Olga remarked that it made all the difference.

"Artistic achievement was more important to me than being commercially successful," said Kathleen. "I spent a lot of time and money creating the cassette. If your tape is good, you'll make your money back. I realized that my cassette would reach a larger audience than my live shows, and it has. You want a product that will still sound good to you in 10 years."

Olga agreed: "That's true. I did a tape of multicultural stories that I thought would sell, but I didn't choose the stories that were important to me. I was so unhappy with the final product that I didn't do another tape for three years. Then I chose the bilingual stories that were part of my heart and soul."

The quality of the final tape can best be tested by listening to it while driving in your car. That's where most people will hear their copies. Can they understand every word?

When it comes to making copies off your master tape, you should make at least 500 at a time for the best cost.

Sandra sells cassettes for several storytellers at festivals and conferences. She understands the J-card (the paper inside the plastic box on which the title and notes of the cassette are printed) can attract a buyer's eye. An action shot of the storyteller telling or an illustration that is bright and simple enough to "read" from a distance are the best.

It's helpful to have your face on the front and to have several colors on your J-card. It's expensive, though. If you can only afford one color besides black, red is good. A good title for your cassette can really help sell it. A big market for your tapes is your own shows and workshops. Most mail-order catalogs and bookstores don't pay for your tapes up front, and generally want 50 to 60 percent of the profits. It can be a real problem waiting for them to pay. One catalog doesn't pay a cent until 12 tapes have been sold. Olga has had a tape listed in their catalog for years, and hasn't seen a cent from them. Find out the payment policy before you send off your tapes.

If a parent books you for a birthday party, you can give one free tape to the child and suggest that the parent purchase tapes for all the other children as party favors. Give a discount, and the parents will be thrilled.

When someone wants information about you, also send them a flier about your tape. When they buy a tape, send them a brochure about yourself. Market yourself when you send the tape, and vice versa.

It now costs Sandra $1.05 for each tape copy, so she gives one to every potential booker and writes it off as advertising expense.

Have a separate account for your tape money. It makes it easier to figure out the sales tax that you must give the state at the end of the year, and you can save profits to help fund your next tape.

When marketing yourself to universities and theaters, send a videotape. Allow them to record your shows, as long as you get a copy of the tape. One way to create an audition tape to send out to bookers is to use recordings made of your tellings and pay a local store to edit snippets together. Do not allow schools or private parties to record, as those tapes are always poorly done.

Olga was very pleased with the videotapes that she recorded with Atlas. She and the other storytellers were firm in asking for a live audience of a wide age range from little children to older adults seated on bleachers, so that they weren't focusing their energy down at listeners seated on the floor. They had three cameras and boom mikes and a very simple background that didn't distract. They insisted that the camera people do no visual stunts or tricks and that no animation be added. The contract was written so the tellers can publish and tell the stories that are on the videos, and three years after the videotapes were made, they can also record their stories again in whatever format they wish. It was written into the contract that the tellers can buy out from the Atlas company any stock that doesn't sell.

Angela recorded some stories with a company that sells multiple-use rights to libraries and other institutions, so they charge $125 for each of her 15-minute videotapes. She gets $7\frac{1}{2}$ percent royalties. Olga gets 3 percent and got an advance of thousands of dollars.

Resources

Awards

Write to the following organizations to learn how to have audiocassettes and video-tapes considered for awards or reviews.

ALA Notable Children's Books and
    Recordings
Association for Library Service to Children
American Library Association
50 East Huron Street
Chicago, IL 60611
Toll free: 800-545-2433, extension 2163

Grammy
National Academy of Recording Arts and
    Sciences
303 North Glen Oaks Boulevard,
    Suite 14 Mez.
Burbank, CA 91502-1178

Indie Awards
NAIRD
P.O. Box 568
Maple Shade, NJ 08052

National Storytelling Association Awards
National Storytelling Association
P.O. Box 309
Jonesborough, TN 37659
Ph: 615-753-2171
Toll free: 800-525-4514

Parents' Choice Awards
Parents' Choice
1191 Chestnut Street
Newton, MA 02164
Ph: 617-965-5913

Storytelling World Awards
ETSU Box 70647
Johnson City, TN 37614

Coach for Producing Tapes

Doug Lipman
P.O. Box 441195
West Somerville, MA 02144
Ph: 617-391-3672
    Doug is a master storyteller with at least 11 tapes. He is available to help with project planning, in-studio coaching, and production and marketing.

Other producers are available, but they have not sent me information as Doug does. (Remember what I said about getting hired— you've got to let potential clients know you're available!) Ask colleagues who have recorded tapes you admire, or write N.S.A.

Catalogs That Sell Audiocassettes of More Than One Storyteller

August House Publishers, Inc.
P.O. Box 3223
Little Rock, AR 72203-3223
Ph: 501-372-5450
Toll free: 800-284-8784
Fax: 501-372-5579

California Storytellers
6695 Westside Road
Healdsburg, CA 95448
Ph: 707-433-8728

E.A.R.S.
12019 Donohue Avenue
Louisville, KY 40243

First Avenue Press
3-1, 550 Beatty Street
Vancouver, BC V6B 2L3
Canada
Ph: 604-688-3086 or 604-738-5335

High Windy Audio
P.O. Box 553
Fairview, NC 28730
Toll free: 800-63-STORY

Invisible Ink: Books on Ghosts & Hauntings
1811 Stonewood Drive
Beavercreek, OH 45432
Toll free: 800-31-GHOST (314-4678)
Fax: 513-429-3823

Ladyslipper
P.O. Box 3124-R
Durham, NC 27715
Ph: 919-683-1570
Toll free: 800-634-6044

National Storytelling Association
P.O. Box 309
Jonesborough, TN 37659
Ph: 615-753-2171
Toll free: 800-525-4514

Stories, Inc.
P.O. Box 20743
Indianapolis, IN 46220
Ph: 317-255-7628

Storylines
P.O. Box 7416
Saint Paul, MN 55107
Ph: 612-643-4321

Weston Woods
389 Newtown Turnpike
Weston, CT 06883
Ph: 203-226-3355
Toll free: 800-243-5020
Fax: 203-226-3818

Sources of Videotapes of Storytellers

Beauty and the Beast Storytellers
P.O. Box 6624
Ithaca, NY 14851
Ph: 607-277-0016

High Windy Audio (See audio listing.)
McDougal Littell
P.O. Box 1667
Evanston, IL 60204
Toll free: 800-323-5435

National Storytelling Association
    (See audio listing.)
Olga Loya
P.O. Box 6482
San Jose, CA 95150
Ph: 408-297-3550

Robert Rubinstein
90 East 49th Avenue
Eugene, OR 97405
Ph: 503-344-8176

Second Story Television
118 East 11 Street, Room 2C
New York, NY 10003
Ph: 212-475-4635

Upstart
32 East Avenue
Hagerstown, MD 21740
Toll free: 800-448-4887

Weston Woods (See audio listing.)

H. W. Wilson Company
950 University Avenue
Bronx, NY 10452
Toll free: 800-367-6770

Tapes Available from the Retreat Discussion Group

The following is a list of the performers who are part of and participate in a retreat discussion group and the audiocassettes each has produced. Call or write these tellers for updated listings of audiocassettes and books, as some of them were working on new projects at the time of this writing.

Angela Lloyd
Kemper Campbell Ranch
Mail Box 4
Victorville, CA 92392
Ph: 619-955-1321
    Dreams and Other Realities: Story Song Poem Chant. At Last Productions, 1995.

Olga Loya
P.O. Box 6482
San Jose, CA 95150
Ph: 408-297-3550
    The Tricks of Life and Death (Las Astuceas de la Vida y la Muerte).
    Storytellers Collection: Tall Tales, Magic Tales, Scary Stories, Animal Stories. (This series is available both as audiocassettes and videotapes. The tellers are Olga Loya, Joe Bruchac, Alice McGill, and Jon Spellman.)

Sandra MacLees
6695 Westside Road
Healdsburg, CA 95448
Ph: 707-433-8728
    Pieces of My Life.
    Sweet and Bittersweet: Tales of Love.

Kathleen Zundell
P.O. Box 66124
Los Angeles, CA 90066
Ph: 310-455 2567
    The Magic Box.
    Snuggle Down Stories.

Further Reading

Apple, Jacki. *Doing It Right in L.A.: Self-Producing for the Performing Artist.* Los Angeles: Astro Artz and Fringe Festival, 1990. Write to: Fringe Festival/Los Angeles, 6380 Wilshire Blvd., Suite 147, Los Angeles, CA 90048.
    How to make a budget, set ticket prices, find a place to perform, promote the event, deal with the media, and handle the door. This book is invaluable for people putting on a concert or festival anywhere in the world.

Black, Judith. "Producing a Tape." *Story Bag: A National Storytelling Newsletter* (October/November 1991, December 1991/January 1992, February/March 1992): 5, 2–3, 2–3.
    How to produce and market a tape and what pitfalls to avoid. An invaluable series by a nationally known storyteller who has produced several award-winning tapes.

Lipman, Doug. *The Storytelling Coach: How to Listen, Praise, and Bring Out People's Best.* Little Rock, AR: August House, 1995.

1995 National Storytelling Directory. Jonesborough, TN: National Storytelling Press, 1994.
    1995 was the first year that articles have been included in the directory. They include: "Nine Steps to a Successful Storytelling Group," "Expert Advice on Planning a Storytelling Event," "The Secret of Getting Sellout Crowds," "Building a Successful Storytelling Venue," "How to Hire a Storyteller," and "Ten Tips Storytellers Wish Sponsors Knew."

Rioux, Terri. "When the Camera's Eye Is on You." *Yarnspinner* (September 1992): 3–4.
    Covers appearing on television or being videotaped.

Sharp, Peggy A. *Sharing Your Good Ideas: A Workshop Facilitator's Handbook*. Portsmouth, NH: Heinemann, 1993.

Sharp takes you step-by-step from choosing a topic through the final evaluation. Every step is full of common-sense advice and practical ideas. Sharp even gives an appendix of ready-to-use forms, charts, and lists that you can use in your next workshop presentation.

Stotter, Ruth. *100 Memorable Quotes About Stories and Storytelling*. Stinson Beach, CA: Stotter Press, 1995.

Here are the quotations that you can use to make points in your workshop.

Weiss, Jim, and Randy Weiss. "The Fine Line Between Good and Excellent in Audio Production." *Yarnspinner* (September 1993): 6–7.

Wilson, Joe, and Lee Udall. *Folk Festivals: A Handbook for Organization and Management*. Knoxville: University of Tennessee Press, 1982.

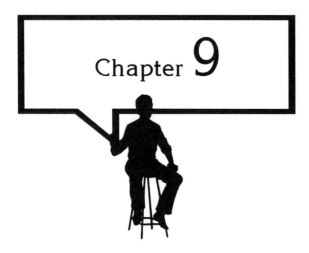

Chapter 9

Money

You will find your most memorable compensation will be the moments when you feel a story sweep through you and into your audience's hearts, but I'm sure you wouldn't be reading this book if you didn't also hope to earn a living.

When determining the fees you will charge, you need to cover your start-up and ongoing costs. School entertainer Chris Holder talks about those ongoing costs in the article reprinted in this chapter. Start-up expenses can range from the cost of a simple business card and phone calls to the costs involved in setting up a home office, buying a computer, taking out ads, purchasing expensive costumes, taking business classes, and attending storytelling festivals all across the country.

Set Reasonable Fees

The following article by Chris Holder, editor of *Artists with Class*, a wonderful newsletter for school performers in New York, provides guidelines for setting your fees.

Set Your Fees for . . . the Decent Buck

Sometimes you may work at rates lower than you prefer. Sometimes you may even agree to work for free or little money if the cause, public relations, or friend is good enough. But if you're a professional independent artist, protect your future just as people with more conventional jobs do.

A conventional job usually pays you a salary every week or two, usually deducts state and federal taxes and social security payments, and often includes such perks as health insurance, disability insurance, retirement, and/or pension plans. Do you include all that when you set your fees?

Suppose you currently charge $250 per day for your work as an artist in the schools. Further suppose you can work 120 days of the 180-day school year and still have enough time to create your art and market yourself successfully. So, you've amassed a gross of $30,000. How does that compare to a teacher who makes $30,000 as his or her annual salary?

Well, you have business expenses that the teacher doesn't have, such as:

1. publicity, printing, photos

2. postage, duplicating, and office supplies

3. owning, operating, maintaining, and insuring a decent business car.

My experience, and that of many of my artist acquaintances is that about one third of your gross will go to pay your expenses, bringing your adjusted gross income down to $20,000. What about sick days, vacation days, and health and disability insurance the teacher receives along with the annual salary? You don't get that, so deduct another $4,000, and bring your total down to $16,000. Now pay your federal, state, local, and social security taxes (almost 15% since you're self-employed—approximately $4,000) which leaves you with an annual professional income of $12,000 and not enough money to heat your home.

Now ask yourself, "Is my gross income of $30,000 and the teacher's salary of $30,000 the same?" Of course not.

But wait! There's another consideration. What about the future? Do you think all your pals down at the local arts council are regularly pouring money into your retirement pension fund for you, carefully guiding and reinvesting your stash to insure its growth at a significantly better pace than inflation? Think again. When your teacher friend retires at 65, she/he will get a gold watch and a monthly check that may be as much as 50% of their final salary. All that you will get will be arthritis.

Independent artists must take the responsibility to set up retirement by investing for themselves. Check with your accountant, tax advisor, or financial advisor and research at the library before investing in the following suggestions:

A. At a bare minimum, open an IRA and contribute $2,000 each year without fail. Do this through a bank CD, stocks, bonds, annuities, or mutual funds.

B. Seriously investigate investing in real estate. This can be as simple as buying your own apartment, condo, house, or perhaps another piece of property which you feel has the potential to increase in value over time. There are special tax advantages to buying, owning, and renting real estate.

C. Invest more funds in a SEP IRA (Simplified Employee Pension Plan) or a KEOGH. You may invest up to 15% of your adjusted income each year and defer its tax until you reach age 62.

D. Investment possibilities are vast. After stocks, bonds, securities, and real estate, you may try precious metals, Broadway shows, inventions—you name it. But be aware that different investments carry different degrees of risk. You must weigh the amount of dollars you can invest against the degree of risk you can tolerate, balanced by your sensible choices that have been based on solid research. Remember, when you're 67, you may not tell stories the way you do now, but you'll still get hungry every day.

So take a look at your own current fee structure, and then try this simple formula:

1. What do you want your adjusted gross income to be (that's line 32 on the federal IRS form)? For this hypothetical example, let's stick with our earlier figure: $30,000.

2. Add a third of that for expenses. (I hope you're thrifty—many businesses require more.) Add $10,000, and you've got $40,000.

3. Add $3,000 for health and disability insurance, sick and vacation days. If you've got a family, it'll cost more, but we'll be conservative here. Now you are up to $43,000.

4. Add $3,000 for all your retirement investments. You'd be safer with at least two grand more per year, but start with $3K this year. New total: $46,000.

5. Now add $2,000 (5% of your gross if you can, but we'll stay conservative again) for "profit to be reinvested in your business/art." Ask an accountant. If you can't do this, you're just treading water. New total: $48,000.

6. Sorry, you've got to pay taxes. Figure $6,000, and add it for your grand total of $54,000.

7. Now divide your gross of $54,000 by the number of days you can work per year (120) to discover that you really should be charging $450 per day, not $250.

Okay, it's facile and contrived. I made it come out even to show that everyone should raise their fees by $200 per day. But the truth is that many independent artists do not include the real expenses of life in their fees. When artists shortchange themselves, sponsors and clients learn to pay too little for quality arts services. Worse, they balk when another comes along legitimately charging much more for similar services. If artists do not learn to value and charge for their work and future, the art-buying public will continue to expect professional arts services at bargain basement prices.

So, find out what you need to make and begin to educate yourself and your clients. If you don't make your needed average over the long haul, you're selling yourself, your fellow storytellers, and your future short.[1]

Where Will They Find Money to Pay You?

This is always a sticky point, but funding can be obtained from a variety of sources, such as the school's parent-teacher group, the state arts council, School Improvement Program (SIP) funds, the friends of the library group, and so on. A local business might agree to donate the dollars. An evening family concert can raise money through ticket sales so that the storyteller can appear at the school during the day for all students. Two schools or libraries in the same area can share the costs and time of a performer. For instance, I charge a flat rate per day to travel to Los Angeles from my home in San Diego. Sometimes two schools will split the fee and my day. I perform at one school in the morning and at the other in the afternoon.

Other schools pay for storytellers by having the artist conduct a weekend or evening workshop for teachers, librarians, parents, other freelance performers, and anyone else willing to pay a small fee to attend.

When traveling to another town for a festival or concert, arrange to tell in other locations in that town. The costs of a plane ticket and room and board can be shared among the bookers or paid by the booker with the most funds.

How to Charge

When a potential booker calls, the first words he or she utters are often, "What do you charge?" This is the toughest question to answer. Do not quote a price until you learn all the details of the booking. Tell the booker that these details affect the fee—and they do. If the booker is planning a party for 200 people in a ritzy section of town, you can charge more than for 10 preschoolers celebrating a birthday in a poorer section.

As you listen, size up the client. Will this person call you several times asking questions about every little detail until you're ready to scream? If so, calculate a "pain-in-the-neck" surcharge into the fee. If the booker insists on setting up a difficult situation for you, such as putting you on opposite the rock band, be sure to charge extra for the stress. Add in the potential costs of long distance phone calls and travel time and expense (for the 1995 tax year, the IRS allowed a $.30/mile business deduction for automobile use).

How should you charge? It depends on the particular booking, but your options include the following:

By the Hour

I personally don't care for the hourly method of calculating fees. We should be paid for the show, and I charge as much for a 10-minute show as for an hour. My overhead is just as costly. My travel time is the same. My booking time for other engagements on the same day is just as limited. I only charge by the hour when giving workshops.

By the Day

You may have a certain fee for a full-day engagement, such as appearing as an artist in a school. It may be more cost-effective for the school to hire you for the day than for just a few assemblies.

By the Head

This method of payment works well with workshops where you are receiving a percentage of the participants' fees. Get an estimate for how many participants there will be, and get a guaranteed minimum fee regardless of the number of participants. You don't want to spend days preparing a two-hour workshop and have only three people show up. If you had arranged to get $5 per person, all your work would net you only $15.

When I perform at coffeehouses where I am to be paid by tip jar donations, my contract stipulates that I will receive at least a minimum payment, which the owners will have to make up out of their own pockets if enough audience members don't ante up. I was glad of that clause the night that I drove 100 miles to a coffeehouse, and only five people showed up. It just so happened that the very same night in the tiny town there was a big party to raise money for a popular man who'd had surgery. Everyone was at the party rather than at my show.

By the Project

This fee arrangement would work for an artist-in-residence. You might charge a certain sum for returning to a location over several weeks or months to do a continuing class, to collect stories to be performed by you or others, or to start a storytelling club or festival.

For Free

If you're working for free, be sure to insist on doing it at your convenience and under the most favorable circumstances. Send the client an invoice detailing your services and the usual fees. Mark the bill "No Charge." This lets your client know that you normally charge for such work. They will value your performance more if they know its monetary worth. Time you give a nonprofit group is not tax-deductible from taxes, only materials are. Check current tax laws with your accountant. You may wish to limit freebies to no more than a few per year. Decide which groups you wish to donate your services to and let them know. If other groups call, put them on a list of charities you will consider for the next year.

If you are making a gift of your services, set clear limits as to exactly what you will and will not do. For example, if you give a friend a coupon good for a free children's birthday show, be sure to put an expiration date on it, state that it is only good for one birthday, and specify the length of the show and the number of children. Some "friends" might be tempted to use a coupon again and again or otherwise abuse your gift.

If you need to turn down a request for voluntary services, you can say, "My time allows for only so much volunteer work, but I will give you a discount."

With a Discount

This is a sticky area. If the booker asks you to do your show for less money, do not give them your full service for the lesser fee. If you agree to a lesser fee, do a shorter show or tell to a smaller group. If you normally have "extras" such as origami, flannel board stories, or handouts, leave them out.

When a member of a small, deserving organization tells me they can't afford my fee, I explain that August and September are my "community service" months, when I will negotiate a lesser price. I've chosen those two months because they are my slowest booking months, so I'm happy to have the work even if I make less money. By calling it a "community service," I don't sound desperate; I sound kind.

By Barter

You can barter your services for a cruise, hotel room, membership in an organization, day at a spa, or entrance to an amusement park. Mother-to-be Cathy Spagnoli told stories at a day care center in Seattle. Every parent that came to the show paid admission with used baby clothes and toys. Barter, though, is considered payment by the IRS, and therefore must be reported.

You can plan an inexpensive vacation to almost anywhere in the United States or abroad by swapping your skills for rooms, and so on. Decide where you want to go on your vacation then research the area's fancy hotels, campgrounds, spas, cruise ships, and recreational trips. Call or write for their brochures. Do they have speakers or entertainment in the evenings? Send them information about yourself as a speaker or entertainer, and offer to trade your services for theirs.

Fees in General

Ask other performers in your area what they charge for various gigs. You may find it varies considerably. I know one storyteller in New York who never charges less than $500. One nationally known performer charges $2,000 for one performance and $7,500 for a one-week residency consisting of three performances and four workshops. Another storyteller who has performed at national festivals still charges only $45 for local library shows because of a well-off spouse. Set your fees at what you think you're worth, but try not to undercut the possibly more experienced competition's prices.

In America, it often seems that people treat you according to what they paid for your services. If they got you for $25, you will be asked to enter the servants' entrance. If they paid $25,000, they will roll out the red carpet. And which fee will you work harder to earn? While we like to think that our worth is not based solely on money, you will undoubtedly find that your attitude about a performance

will also depend in part on what you are paid. When I was added as an artist to the Orange County Performing Arts Center's roster, I was paid three times what I had been charging by myself. Now, when I perform in Orange County, I can charge much more than my usual rate. However, in San Diego County I still charge less than the Center would, so the bookers feel they're getting a bargain, and I'm getting a raise.

Raise your fees every year to keep up with the cost of living and any increase in demand for your services. For this reason, never put your prices on your brochures. If you do publish a price list, be sure to clearly list the expiration date of the prices. If you don't, three years later a copy will land in the hands of someone who wishes to book you at the old prices.

Are you getting every gig you try for? If so, it's time to raise your prices. It's normal for some bookers to insist that you are charging too much. If they say they have to check with a committee or another person before they can confirm you, ask for the contact's phone number, and set a date by which the booker will either confirm or cancel. If they don't call by that date, call them. If they cancel because of your high price, ask what they would have been willing to pay—just for your own information. The best reason to lose a job is because your price is too high.

Once you've set your fees, there's still the small matter of making sure that you actually get them. When arranging a performance, find out exactly where, to whom, and when to submit your invoice. If you can send it directly to the department or person who will send your check, you might receive your payment more quickly. Find out when you should receive payment and whom to call if you don't receive it.

Not Being Paid

While you may have to wait for payment from bookings, your mortgage, grocery bills, and other expenses won't wait. Therefore, it's important that you keep track of who owes you payment and when you should receive it. Getting paid can be a tricky proposition.

When you are handed a sealed envelope with your payment, resist the urge to merely slip it into a pocket or a purse. Open the envelope before the booker leaves, verify the amount, and ensure that the check is signed.

I've been given several unsigned checks, although unintentionally.

Many performers require a (often nonrefundable) deposit or even the total amount of their fee before they will tell. Others insist on cashier's checks or even cash. If the grapevine says that a booker is unreliable, get payment far enough in advance to ensure the check clears your bank before the show. If the booker's check is returned for non-sufficient funds, your bank will penalize you.

IRS Deductions

It is a good idea to talk to a tax consultant now to find out what business-related tax deductions you will be allowed to take. Find out right away, because you must back up any deductions with records. Keep track of all your income and expenses. I have a notebook with several pockets in it. Whenever I pay for anything that can be deducted—stamps, bulk mail permits, photocopying, office supplies, stationery, brochures, photographs, business cards, computer programs, books and cassettes for research, costumes, sound equipment, advertisements, booth space at a conference, meals and lodging on overnight business trips, state and city taxes, airline tickets to a gig, and so on—I put the receipts in the appropriate pocket. Then when tax time rolls around, I can start adding up how much I've spent. It helps me figure out my expenses for my own information as well as for the government's. The staggering truth is that I

spend more than $1,000 each year on postage alone!

If you have an office in your home, figure out the percentage of total square feet of your dwelling that it takes up. You can write off the same percentage of your house mortgage interest or apartment rental and your utilities as a deduction. You may also write off any business calls made, but if you use the same phone line for business and personal calls, note in your appointment book the time, the phone number, who you called, and for what purpose. Keep all your phone company bills. Check with your tax advisor, though, to be sure you qualify for a home office deduction; the IRS's rules are very restrictive, and declaring a home office can increase your chances of an audit.

Also check with your tax accountant to see if you should also be writing off your mileage to business-related locations, such as the office supplies store, the library, and places where you are putting on shows. If so, your accountant can tell you how to document your expenses and which method of calculation to use.

I highly recommend hiring a tax preparer to file your return because of the many forms and rules that apply to the self-employed, and the changes that the IRS makes annually. Of course, the advice in this section is meant to serve as general information and is not guaranteed.

Performance and Pay

I once met a teller who said scornfully to a group of freelance professionals, "I am not one of those tellers who tells to make a living. I live to tell." Her implication was that because we are concerned about our fees, we couldn't possibly care about the stories and the audiences. I then observed her begin her workshop by complaining that she wasn't being paid to give it. This made some participants feel guilty. It was very unprofessional behavior.

Whether you are being paid or performing for free, put as much effort into every show as if you were making a million dollars. Every audience deserves the best, and every performance and workshop is an audition to potential bookers or friends of potential bookers. Never discuss your fee or complain that you are not being paid adequately. Set your fees at a rate that pays you reasonably well for your artistry, time, and expenses. Do a performance worthy of that fee, and bookers will be happy to pay it.

Resources

Periodicals

Artists with Class. Quarterly. To subscribe, write Chris Holder, 66 Jenkins Road, Burnt Hills, NY 12027, or phone 518-399-3135. The 1995 subscription rate was $12.

Further Reading

Messman, Carla. *The Artist's Tax Guide and Financial Planner, 1992.* New York: Lyons & Burford, 1991.

How to set up your books, keep receipts and records, and report to the IRS.

Wellner, Cathryn. "Get Your Prices Up." *Story Bag: A National Storytelling Newsletter* (October/November 1993): 4–6.

Seven ploys bookers will use in negotiating fees (or the lack thereof) with you, and seven reasons why you should charge what you're worth!

Notes

1. Chris Holder, "Set Your Fees for . . . the Decent Buck," *Artists with Class*, 11 (Fall, 1987): 2. Reprinted with permission.

Chapter 10

Contracts and Agreements

I've always liked to assume that people are basically honest, so for many years I didn't bother with a contract, and the only time in the first nine years of my professional storytelling career that I didn't receive the full amount I was promised, I had a contract. The booker declared bankruptcy.

Then two incidents showed me that a contract should always be used because it serves as a means of clear communication as well as a legal document.

In the first incident, a parent volunteer and I agreed over the telephone on my fee for some assemblies. When the check arrived a month after my shows, however, the amount was less than our agreement. The principal had authorized payment according to a fee schedule that was several years old. This misunderstanding could have been avoided if I'd had my fee included in a contract. The incident also taught me to include in my fee schedules the dates the prices go into effect and when they expire.

The second mix-up occurred when a teaching assistant at a university called for her professor. I told the student that I would only charge half my normal fee because the gig was in August, my community service month. I told my stories to the delight of children and staff, then asked the professor if the check would be mailed to me. She looked shocked and said that her understanding was that I had volunteered my services. I explained that I had a four-year policy of never performing for free for anyone. The teaching assistant insisted that I had agreed to charge nothing. Because the student seemed upset, I kindly said that the confusion was partly my fault because I hadn't sent a contract. That night the student called me to announce that the professor and she had agreed that they had no obligation to pay me because I had no contract! Now I send a contract for every booking.

Fees are not the only thing that needs to be verified in a contract to prevent misunderstandings. The dates and times of your shows, the type of stories you will perform, the directions to the location, and any special requirements you have, such as a microphone on a stand, should be verified and agreed upon in writing. If a booker tells you to turn right when they meant to say "left"—or if you write down "right" when they said "left"—you might get lost, leading to a postponement or a cancellation of your show. The bookers will assume that the confusion was your fault—unless you produce a signed contract that has all the details written out, including the incorrect information. With any luck, your bookers will read the contracts you send before signing them, preventing these mistakes from the start.

When I began having problems with last-minute cancellations in 1995 as schools and teachers ran out of funds before my visit, I changed my contract to require a deposit at the time of the booking. The deposit is nonrefundable if the show is canceled with less than a month's notice.

A Sample Contract

I customize my contracts according to my needs and those of the booker. Following is a sample of my contract.

Storyteller Harlynne Geisler

Performance Confirmation

Organization's Name _____

Organization's Phone _____

Representative _____

Representative's Phone (day & night) _____

Address _____

City _____ State _____ Zip_____

Performance Date(s) _____

Times of Shows [*Ages of children at each show to be noted, if applicable*]

_____

_____

Performance Location & Directions _____

_____

_____

Instructions for Schools:

The school agrees to provide a microphone on a skinny metal stand or a wireless microphone—please set it up half an hour before my show so that I can test it. The children will be seated in rows on the floor. IMPORTANT: Do not make any changes in the show times or the ages of children to be present at a particular show without first calling the Storyteller and asking for approval of the changes. PLEASE be sure to tell all teachers and the principal this. [*I used to put this note in the instructions at the bottom of the contract. The truth is most people do not read those instructions. Any important information should be in the body of the contract.*]

Performance Instructions for Other Organizations (Such as Clubs):

If there is a big room with everyone scattered around at tables, or if there is to be more than 100 listeners, a microphone on a skinny metal stand or a wireless microphone is required. If a wireless mike is to be used, please inform the Storyteller at least two days before. [*This requirement about notification is so that I can wear a dress that has a belt or a pocket to hold the battery pack.*] Please be sure that any noisy distractions are kept to a minimum.

Performance Fee:

$ _____ . A deposit of 25% of fee must accompany this confirmation with the rest to be paid at the time of the show. This deposit is nonrefundable if the show(s) are canceled with less than a 30-day notice.

Organization Representative's Signature:

_____

Date:

_____

Storyteller's Signature:

_____

Date:

_____

Instructions:

Please sign and date this contract and return it with the deposit to Harlynne Geisler in the enclosed envelope. [*I always send a stamped, self-addressed envelope along with the two copies.*] Keep a copy for your files. If you have any questions, call Harlynne Geisler immediately. [*Be sure your name and address is on your contract so they can get in touch with you if necessary.*]

Duplication Policy:

The Booker agrees that no part of the performance shall be recorded or allowed to be recorded on videotape, audio tape, or any other duplication process without the prior written consent of the Storyteller.

Cancellation Policy:

Should the Booker decide to cancel with less than a 30-day notice to the Storyteller, except in the case of natural disasters such as fire or earthquake, the deposit will not be refunded. [*Your cancellation and deposit policy may be different.*]

Publicity Policy for Clubs, Libraries, Festivals, Etc.:

The Booker agrees that any printed material developed to advertise the show—such as notices in newsletters, advertisements, fliers, press releases, posters, programs, and brochures—will include Harlynne Geisler's name *spelled correctly* and specifically mention storytelling. Two copies of any such promotional material will be sent to Harlynne Geisler. [*It's very important to see if the description that actually goes out to the public about what you'll be doing matches what you plan to do. Otherwise the audience may have expectations you know nothing about and may not be satisfied with your performance. I use the publicity materials that are sent to me for résumés, press kits, scrapbooks, etc.*]

Harlynne Geisler

5361 Javier Street, San Diego, CA 92117-3215 (619) 569-9399

Jim Kleefeld's *The Contract Book* and *The Booking Notebook* are invaluable aids to the beginning professional. I developed my own contracts from the many sample contracts in his book. Before I had a computer, I did as he suggested: just pasted my letterhead at the top of his samples, photocopied them, and filled in the blanks with the information for each show. (See the "Resources" section at the end of this chapter for ordering information.)

Videotaping or Audiotaping Requests

Bookers often ask me if they can tape my shows. It's a good idea to find out why the person or organization or school wishes to do so. I once had a doting grandfather videotape my show for a sick child. Of course, I gave him permission. I also allow videotaping of snippets of stories for the video scrapbook kept at some schools.

However, some people intend to use tapes of my performances in place of hiring me in the future. "I'm planning on putting it in the district library to be checked out," one booker told me. To protect myself from losing bookings in this way, I came up with the following videotape agreement (at bottom of page), which you might adapt for yourself.

The booker must sign and date this contract and provide an address. If I haven't received my copy of the tape in 10 days, I write the booker to void the contract.

The reason that I ask that the tape be erased within a year is that I live on my return bookings. Of course, I always have a new show and never repeat any stories unless specifically asked to, but this keeps the tape from being used for classes years after I've been there.

If you notice people for whom you've not granted permission with cameras or tape recorders, quietly explain to them, "I'm performing copyrighted material, and I only have permission to do it live, with the understanding that any recording of this material would require additional permission and a fee paid." This makes it sound like it's the holders of the copyright who are the bad guys, not you. The taper doesn't need to know for which material you hold the copyright.

These days tape recorders are so small that some people will tape without asking your permission and without your knowledge. Once, I had an older mother tell me she had taped me for her daughter who was undergoing painful cancer treatment. "Your stories will help her forget her pain for a little while," she said. Again, of course, I didn't ask her to erase the tape.

This videotape made of Harlynne Geisler performing and/or conducting a workshop will:

1. Be copied, and the copy sent to Ms. Geisler at her office within 10 days, OR the rest of this agreement is void.

2. Be used only at the school or by the organization who hired Ms. Geisler.

3. Not be used in any way to replace a live performance or workshop by Ms. Geisler.

4. Be used for only one year before being erased.

5. Not be used for profit in any way.

Resources

Further Reading

Kleefeld, Jim. *The Booking Notebook*. Avon, OH: Contemporary Magic, 1988.

A complete booking system that includes show booking sheets and checklists in a loose-leaf notebook, plus a section providing advice on booking shows. Write to 33510 Jennie Road, Avon, OH 44011-2042.

———. *The Contract Book*. Avon, OH: Contemporary Magic, 1988.

A compendium of contracts and contract information for entertainers, including a variety of reproducible contract forms.

Chapter **11**

Organizing Your Time, Your Office, and Your Research

Some people tell me that I am the most organized person they know. I look around my office and my computer room at the piles with the mental labels of "To Do: Learn, Write, Call, and/or Decide," "To Be Filed in My Left-Hand Filing Cabinet," "To Be Filed in My Right-Hand Filing Cabinet," "To Be Filed in My Closet," "To Be Filed in My Desk," "To Be Thrown Out If Only I Had the Courage," and "Anonymous" (piles that haven't been looked at in so long that I've forgotten what they are) and laugh hollowly at the thought.

Nonetheless, I am glad that I am at least halfway organized. Some performers feel that because they are "artistes," they are above such mundane things as contracts, showing up for bookings on time, collecting receipts for tax purposes, or other bourgeois tasks. However, "artistes" generally starve and are often a pain in the neck to their bookers.

If you want to save money by earning tax deductions, prevent stress caused by bookers who had a different understanding of your obligations than you did, and save time searching for the perfect story for a performance, then get organized!

All of the following ideas are not meant to be implemented tomorrow. After all, I'm not trying to add to your stress. These are suggestions that can be tried out, revised, or discarded over a long period of time.

Setting Goals

Having goals—lifetime, five-year, one-year, even daily—helps. You can't get where you wish to go if you aren't aimed in that direction. The German proverb puts it best: What's the use of running if you're not on the right road? Story coach Doug Lipman would add that it's important to remember that the road will come to many forks where your goals can be changed.

At the annual storyteller's retreat that I attend, we always write down personal, professional, and artistic goals for the next day, week, and year, for our lifetimes, and if we only had six months left to live. That last set of goals can help clarify what is really important to you.

If you plan to borrow money to achieve your career goals, write a business plan with the following sections: a description of your business and its products and services; a marketing plan for how you intend to get bookings and sell your products; and a financial plan. Knowing your goals will help you plan for the success of your business.

Daily and Weekly Goals

What small everyday goals have you set for yourself? Do you want to work on voice and breath control every day or several times a week? How often will you exercise, pray, or meditate so you'll be in shape for storytelling? How often will you set aside time to do various business chores such as filing, making phone calls, and bringing your accounts up to date? How much time will you spend researching and rehearsing? If you make all these things part of your week, they will become habit.

Yearly Goals

Look at your bookings calendars for the past several years. Is there a pattern to when you are hired? Are there slow periods that you need to save for during the busy times? Are there times that you could be working more if you tried harder? For example, do you put on a wonderful Christmas show suitable for private parties, but only get one party booking for the whole month of December? Then one of your annual goals might be to get the word out about your holiday program.

Maybe you get plenty of calls to do Christmas shows but feel your stories are weak. Make it one of your annual goals to research and rehearse new holiday tales well in advance of December, such as August.

If you have a part-time or full-time job other than storytelling, decide how you can fit storytelling into your year. When I was working for a public library on Mondays and Wednesdays, I could rehearse and tell stories on other days. If there was a particular booking on a Monday or Wednesday that I really

wanted to do, I could use my vacation time from the library. If you work for a school, you can tell evenings, weekends, and vacations as well as telling as part of your school job.

Plan personal goals as well. Do you want to block out certain days or weeks during the year for vacations or other important events? Don't take bookings during those time periods unless you absolutely must. I plan my vacations during slow booking periods.

Break your long-term goals into smaller more specific goals that can be attained in the short term. Let's say that your goal for the next year is to make an audiocassette of your stories. That's the general goal. Specific, short-term goals include choosing your theme and stories, determining your audience, getting permission to tell copyrighted stories, rehearsing and timing your performance, researching recording studios and the costs of duplication, designing a J-card and flier, saving or borrowing money to make the tape, recording the stories, duplicating the master tape, and marketing and selling the cassettes.

Lifetime

Every freelance storyteller probably has the same general lifetime professional goals: developing a large repertoire of finely crafted and unique tales, becoming well-known and respected, and making a decent living from their art. Storytellers who have full- or part-time careers in another field would probably add the goal of balancing storytelling with their other jobs and their families.

My lifetime goals include staying healthy, having enough money to retire comfortably, and not pushing myself too hard as I get older. In my thirties, my lifetime goal was to become a storytelling superstar. Now that I'm in my forties, my priorities have changed, and I have become more realistic. Now my professional goals are to be the best storyteller I can, not to compare myself to other performers, and to travel to other states several times each year.

Making Time

"But I haven't got the time!" We have all used that excuse at some time, but it's just an excuse. At a workshop conducted by author Jane Yolen, someone asked her how she had raised three children and still managed to write so many books. Jane replied that she hadn't waited around for the time fairy to hit her on the head with a magic wand. Instead she had just made the time.

We all get only 24 hours in a day and have our own priorities for how we use that time. In the next section, I share some of the ways that I make my time count double. Maybe some of these tricks can work for you.

Finding, learning, and rehearsing stories takes a lot of time. I often choose my stories on the basis of how many shows the story will fit. For example, when I was planning my "Woof! Dog Tales Around the World" show for the public libraries, I looked for a dog story that I could also tell it at the Scottish Highland Games. The story I found was a Scottish tale about the ghost of a dog, so it was great for Halloween, too. I also use it when I lecture on folktales. One story that serves four purposes—perfect!

These other methods will help you fit stories into your busy day.

- Listen to story tapes you've made, bought, or borrowed:

  while driving in your car.

  while doing exercises, such as walking, by wearing headphones and a small portable cassette player.

  while doing chores at home that require no special mental effort, such as washing dishes or straightening up the garage.

- Read a story:

  while standing in line at the bank, the amusement park, the movie theater, and so on. The average American will spend five years out of a lifetime standing in line, so always have a story with you. When you get to the front of the line, mark where you stopped reading, so you can take up where you left off in the next line.

  while taking a bath, brushing your teeth, and so on. The bathroom can truly become the reading room if you keep a rack of magazines, books, and story photocopies in it.

- Practice your story:

  silently while standing in all those lines.

  out loud to a willing child or adult listener in long lines. Not only will you entertain them, you might amuse eavesdroppers.

  while exercising.

  while doing chores.

  with family, friends, colleagues, neighborhood children, religious groups, organizations to which you belong, and so on. Sometimes this will take the more informal shape of talking about the story rather than telling it. As we all know, sometimes our nearest and dearest don't expect to sit and respectfully listen to you. They expect to have a conversation, so discuss the story with them. It may provide you with new insights.

Discipline

Goals don't get accomplished without discipline. Storytelling can involve a lot of traveling, but it also requires much time spent in a home office. Working out of your home means that you have to keep distractions to a minimum. This can be difficult.

Often friends and family believe that because you are home, you're free at any time to chitchat or perform favors. To prevent interruptions, set up "office hours" during which you don't want to be disturbed and inform everyone who might call or drop by. If these people persist in coming over or phoning, use your answering machine to screen your calls, park your car in the garage, and don't answer the door during your business hours.

If the television and kitchen are luring you away from that new story you were going to write, empty the house of tempting food. Disable or remove the television. If that isn't an option, and you can't resist the temptations, you may have to leave your home. Research and writing can be done at the library. Rehearsal can be done in a quiet corner of a public park.

Don't procrastinate. When someone asks me to develop a handout or make a contract, I try to do it within the same hour or at least on the same day that I receive the request. If you can't work that quickly, set a deadline for yourself and put it on your calendar.

Organizing Your Office

There are many books on running a home office. Your office might be a corner of the kitchen table or a separate room complete with computer and copy machine. How organized do you have to be? If you only have a show or workshop once or twice a month and you've had no trouble getting to the bookings, taking along the materials you've promised, and getting paid, then you've probably already worked out a system that fits your needs. As you expand the number of bookings and find yourself frantically trying to remember details at the last minute—well then, it's time to get more organized.

At the very least you should keep a calendar or appointment book and have an answering machine to take messages when you're not home. If you have children or other people in your home, train them to answer the phone in a pleasant manner and to write down complete messages. An impatient teenager who forgets to pass on messages can cost you business.

Organizing Your Desk

You want to sound professional and prepared when people call. In chapter 5 I covered some of the questions you and the caller will want answered. Your desk should have all the tools you need to answer the caller's questions and with which to record the answers to your own questions.

The booker will want to know if you are available at a certain date and time, so keep your appointment calendar handy. I also have my latest fee schedule posted near my desk, so I can be sure to quote the correct prices, and keep my file boxes of index cards with notes about previous bookings on the desk, so I can quickly refresh my memory about how much I was paid the last time I performed for the booker, when I was there, and what I did. I can then refer to these facts during the conversation. For example, I might be able to tell the principal that I've already given two Halloween assemblies at her school, but that her students would enjoy my December holiday tales and that my fee is the same as it was two years ago.

I also have a fairly elaborate system for keeping track of potential bookers, tentative bookings, confirmed bookings, and information to be mailed.

Storyteller Marilyn McPhie is more casual in her organization. She uses only one file folder and puts all of her notes and phone messages in it in no particular order. She writes her engagements on a calendar in her kitchen. Her system wouldn't work for me, but Marilyn has had no trouble finding her information and showing up for all bookings.

Heather Forest, however, is more organized because she is more tightly booked and travels more than either Marilyn or me. Heather has a loose-leaf binder and moves each booking sheet from section to section in the binder as she goes through the booking process. The sheet starts in the query section, moves to the tentative booking section, and ends up in the confirmed booking section. Each section is ordered by date.

Keeping Files

If you teach storytelling workshops and classes, you will develop handouts for your students. Start keeping files of all the storytelling information you find in articles, bibliographies, catalogs, newsletters and periodicals, and handouts and brochures from other storytellers. Someday you will be able to use this information to help you create original materials that draw upon all you have learned.

Contracts

After every performance, I staple any notes about the show or the booker to my copy of the contract and file them for future reference. You might find yourself referring to a past contract to see what you charged a particular booker, or to confirm which year you were last there, or for any number of other reasons.

Computer Files

Many of my files and contracts are now on computer. All of my files are backed up onto floppy diskettes in case of a hard disk failure, and every six months I copy all of my new or revised files onto diskettes, which I store in a safe deposit box at the bank. Each diskette is labeled, and I have made an index to the diskettes and an alphabetical list of files with their diskette location. Yes, it has been difficult to get this system up and running, but I have 150 diskettes, and it would be a real pain to have to look at the labels on each of those diskettes every time I was trying to locate a single file.

Directions

I have two files of directions. One is just for schools because I perform at so many of them. The other is for all other bookings.

I always note the number of miles and length of driving time on written directions so I can plan my drive when I return to that location.

Handouts

Whenever I create handouts for a workshop or lecture, I keep my originals in a file so that they will be easy to find and duplicate for the next booking.

Letters

I have corresponded with people from every state and province in North America as well as a few foreign countries. I keep all of this correspondence on file. Whenever I am going to be traveling somewhere, I pull out the file on that area and write everyone who has ever gotten in touch with me to ask if they can get me bookings. It didn't work for my trip to Florida, but it did get me bookings on my trips to Illinois and Texas. Make sure the letter you are filing has the date and the return address on it for future reference.

Records of Previous Shows

Nothing would be more embarrassing than returning to a location, starting to tell a story, and having your audience tell you that you told that same tale the last time you performed for them. While some will enjoy hearing it again, others will wonder if you have such a limited repertoire that you must repeat the same stories again. Keeping a record of which stories were told will prevent that problem.

Stories

I have one file drawer for nothing but photocopies of stories that I hope to learn someday. I organize them into different files by topic.

Thanks

Save all the letters of recommendations and thank-you notes that you receive from adults and any interesting ones from children. When every child in an elementary school class sends you a picture and a thank-you note, at first you'll keep them all until they number in the hundreds. Then you'll start being selective.

Your Storytelling Scrapbooks

A storytelling scrapbook is a good idea for every professional storyteller. Start one now, whether you just tell stories occasionally as a sideline or you've been a pro for 10 years. Put programs, fliers, and newspaper clippings into the scrapbook. Be sure to date all the materials.

I've been keeping a scrapbook for 15 years and have filled four three-ring binders.

Your scrapbook can be useful in three ways: to preserve memories, to use as a résumé, and to show as a portfolio.

The memories are for you, as most personal scrapbooks are. You can also share them with friends and family, telling funny and touching anecdotes about various performances.

A résumé in some form is required of all professional tellers. Program directors will want a short biography to print in their publicity. Emcees will want to know what to say in an introduction. People will write asking about your experience as a teller. Most brochures and fliers put out by tellers include a list of places where they have performed. Your scrapbook will help you compose any form of résumé you may need.

A portfolio is used by other professionals to show their backgrounds. You can use it during interviews with program directors. For instance, one events coordinator wanted to see what sort of costumes I had used in the past so she could choose the one she wanted me to wear for her show. I was able to show her pictures from my scrapbook that answered her questions.

Organizing Your Library

I have four bookcases crammed with books in my home office, and my storytelling library would be a lot larger if I didn't live a mile from a public library. At first my books were in no special order at all, but I got tired of searching for the one I needed, so I created a simple system for organizing my library. I looked at all my books and saw that they naturally fell into broad categories, such as folktales, literature, writing, and storytelling. But those categories were still too broad. Often when I do a show, I want to include an Asian, an African or African-American, a Hispanic, and a European or European-American folktale. However, I have more than 300 books of folklore, and it would take much too long to search that many books looking for a specific culture. I began to separate my folklore books by culture. I organized the rest of my library in a similar manner, and now I can easily find my books on any subject.

You may prefer to organize your books alphabetically, by author, or according to the Dewey decimal system.

My audiocassettes are arranged by the teller's last name in a separate bookcase. I have entered their names into my computer and keep a hard copy of the file near the cassettes so that I can scan it quickly to find tapes. I have so few storytelling records, CDs, and videotapes that they don't need to be organized, yet.

Organizing Your Research

Perhaps all of your stories are your own fictional creations, or completely autobiographical . If so, your research may be limited to checking spelling and pronunciation and some investigation into other time periods and cultures. However, if your stories are memories and folktales collected from your family or people in a particular group, such as residents of a nursing home or Vietnamese immigrants, you may also want to learn how to interview people.

Many tellers weave personal experiences and folklore together. They may create shows around themes. Explore your library to find the books you will find most useful as sources and in finding and researching the kinds of tales you want to tell. While there is no single book that I believe every storyteller must have, I do find having my own copy of Margaret MacDonald's *The Storytellers' Sourcebook* invaluable. When you find yourself going to the public library again and again to use the same book, it may be time to purchase your own copy.

No matter how large your book and tape collection, the public library will continue to be the best resource for research. However, public libraries are always in danger of funding cuts. Join your local Friends of the Library and help raise money to preserve this important resource.

Organizing Your Stories

When you find a story you want to learn, make a record of it. I do so on index cards and in my computer. I make note of the sources where I found the story, and of such information as general topics, length of the performance, and potential audiences. Here is a sample of a typical story card:

Sample Card—Front

Title: "The Knee-High Man"

Culture: African-American

Length: 5 minutes

Story Outline:
The Knee-High Man wants to be bigger
asks Ms. Horse—says eat corn & run
asks Mr. Bull—says eat grass & bellow

Sample Card—Back

Story Outline (cont.):
Ms. Owl asks why wants to be bigger
K.H. Man says to fight and to see far
Owl says never get in fights & can climb tree
to see, says he wanted what he didn't need

Sources:

The Knee-High Man and Other Tales. Julius Lester. New York: Dial, 1972.

The Book of Negro Folklore. Langston Hughes and Arna Bontemps. New York: Dodd, Mead, 1958.

Keep your story cards in a file box. When you're looking for a good story from a particular culture, about a specific subject, or to fill in a specific amount of time, check your cards. For example, "The Knee-High Man" could be used to celebrate Black History Month, to make a point about how we don't have to let handicaps limit our lives, to complement a program about farms, or to fill the last five minutes of a family show.

If it's been a year since you last shared the story, read the summary to refresh your memory. If you want to look at your sources again, use the card to relocate them.

Organizing your time, office, and research will allow you to enjoy your storytelling more, and help prevent mistakes and misunderstandings. Some of these problems will be discussed in the next chapter.

Resources

Further Reading

Cooney, Catherine. "Using Your Computer to Organize Your Repertoire." *Storytelling Magazine* (July 1994): 23.

Grayzel, Eva. "Compiling a Storyteller's Log." *Storytelling Magazine* (July 1994): 22–23.

MacDonald, Margaret. *The Storyteller's Sourcebook: A Subject, Title, and Motif Index to Folklore Collections for Children.* Detroit: Gale, 1982.

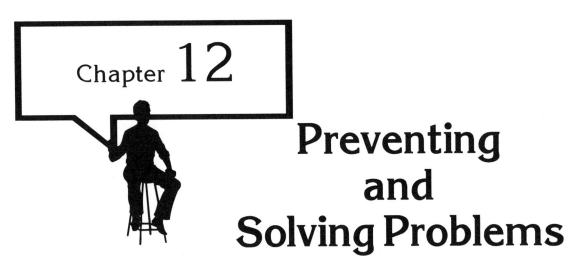

Chapter **12**

Preventing and Solving Problems

Trust in God—but tie your camel tight.
—Persian proverb

The next two chapters were easy for me to write because in my 16 years as a freelance teller, I've faced every challenge and made every mistake possible! If you've had trouble, don't beat yourself up. Consider it one of life's learning experiences. Then brainstorm about how you will prevent such problems from happening again.

The Tale of the Wise Fool

Everyone knows that Nasreddin was a wise fool of whom many tales are told in the Middle East. You say you didn't know that? Well then, I'll tell you a story about him, and you will.

Nasreddin was asked to give the sermon at the local mosque for three Fridays in a row.

Being a lazy man, he hadn't prepared his talk by the time the first Friday rolled around. Looking at the congregation, he asked, "Good people, do you know what I'm going to tell you today?"

"No, Nasreddin," replied the men seated on the prayer rugs.

"No, Nasreddin," whispered the women hidden behind the lattice-work in the balcony.

"What? Well, if you're so ignorant, I can't be bothered to share my knowledge," huffed Nasreddin. He stalked out of the mosque.

The next Friday he asked the same question. This time the cunning congregation, remembering the week before, called out, "Yes, Nasreddin!"

"Then I won't waste your time telling you what you already know." Nasreddin smiled and walked out.

On the third Friday when Nasreddin repeated his question, the congregation was so confused that some answered "Yes" and some answered "No."

"Good," beamed Nasreddin. "Let the people who know tell the people who don't." And he strolled out of the mosque to go home and lie under his fig tree.

The End 📖

This story illustrates how Nasreddin handled his problem. Have you thought of how you'll handle yours? (By the way, this is a good story with which to start a lecture or workshop on storytelling.)

One Show—Preparation vs. Reality

I'm a belt-and-suspenders' person. In other words, I try to prepare for all possibilities, always expecting either my suspenders to snap or my belt to break. Of course, the reality is that it is impossible to control the universe, even one small show. Nonetheless, I continue to try.

Once I told spooky stories to 600 teenage Girl Scouts at a camp. I had an outdoor stage, a captive audience with no competition for entertainment, and a large repertoire of stories in a subject (spooky stories) that is always a crowd-pleaser. The program went over so well that the Girl Scouts called me up when the headquarters was planning their Cookie Sale Kick-Off at Sea World. I was to perform for 5,000 Girl Scouts before they watched the whale show.

I did a lot of research at the library, looking for a story that could incorporate whales, dolphins, and cookies. I found an American folk tale about a mermaid who makes kelp pies for a whale she loves who has her friends the lobsters and clams hold onto the whale's tail while she tries to give him a kiss. I changed the kelp pies into seaweed cookies, and the lobsters and clams into dolphins. Then I added participation words, noises, and gestures, and I was set. I rehearsed the story endlessly, writing it, recording it, practicing it alone, on my husband Jud, and with several different classes at schools I visited. I asked the students to evaluate the story honestly, and through their reactions and comments I refined the story and my presentation. But in spite of all of my preparation, things started going wrong right away.

The venue was the Shamu Stadium at Sea World, and I wasn't allowed on the stage because my presence would confuse the whales. Instead I had to stand in front of the whale tank, almost in the bleachers themselves. There was no platform to raise me up, and a curved set of bleachers that extended so far on either side of me that I was unable to see the audience seated on the ends.

Because my performance was to be filmed and shown on the giant screen above the stage, I had to change into brighter clothes and perform with my head tilted at a strange angle. I was unable to get a sound check, or even to find out in advance what kind of a microphone I would be using. The promotional materials didn't mention me by name, even though that was a stipulation of the contract.

When I was introduced, the emcee left out the line in my introduction that instructed the scouts to welcome me by applauding, so I walked up to the podium in dead silence . . . to be met by a technician taping a working microphone to the malfunctioning one already on the podium.

During the performance, girls who saw themselves shown on the big screen stopped listening and began mugging for the camera. Whenever a whale appeared in the tank behind us, the emcee lost the audience's attention while they stamped their feet chanting "Shamu, Shamu." To top things off, a mime that I hadn't been told was scheduled began mimicking me during my act.

Still, I had prepared myself with relaxation and breathing exercises, and I proceeded with the show. My words echoed back at me because of the sound equipment, which I hadn't been able to rehearse with. My show went long because of the feedback and the enthusiastic audience participation in my first story, so my audience became distracted and impatient for the main event.

As difficult as that show was, though, one scout leader said to me with surprise in her tone, "I really liked your stories!" Then, in the week after my show, I appeared at several schools and ran into Girl Scouts who had enjoyed my tales at Sea World. It was wonderful to be asked at the last school to "tell that whale story again." I guess I did some things right! After that, I had to put my Sea World experience aside mentally so I could concentrate on rewriting Alice in Wonderland for a birthday party the very next week. That's the great thing about storytelling—there's always another challenge ahead.

Handling Challenges

Fortunately, it's rare to have so many problems to deal with in one show. In this chapter I offer some suggestions for coping with or avoiding some of these issues.

When the Big Audience Doesn't Come

Sometimes it takes more energy to captivate a tiny group than a large group. This is because the audience's attention and response feeds energy back to the performer, who then feeds it back to the group. Even if my audience is smaller than expected, though, I do the full show that I've been contracted for unless the bookers indicate that they prefer a shorter program. And even if it takes more effort, I perform as enthusiastically as if the audience were 100 strong.

Once I went to a comedy club on a slow night. There were only five tables of people in the whole place. The four comedians that night attacked us verbally, as if it was our fault that there weren't more people! I thought to myself, You've just ensured that we don't come back and that we don't bring our friends to hear you. If the comedians' attitudes and words had made the audience feel good about showing up, I might have had an entirely different response.

Refer back to chapter 5 for additional information on how to attract an audience.

When Audience Members Are Disruptive

One benefit of storytelling is that you probably won't have to handle disruptions very often. You'll soon find a real difference in your audience's attention span when listening to a story as opposed to when they are listening to you explain the story or storytelling. When you lecture, you are asking your listeners to use the logical side of their brains.

When you tell a story, you are asking them to use logic to understand the words, but also their imaginations to project ahead and "see" the characters, setting, and actions; their memory to recollect what happened before this moment in the story; and their emotions to respond to the story characters. In other words, story listening is a whole-brain activity. Because of this total engagement, audience members seem to be truly "entranced," or hypnotized, by the magic of a good story. Oklahoma storyteller Fran Stallings first alerted me to this.

If some listeners are misbehaving, it's best not to step out of the role of teller into that of disciplinarian. Don't snap sharply, "Stop that!"—it will destroy the story magic and make it hard for you and the audience to sink back into the tale. Instead, try eye contact and a slight shake of the head, a gentle pressure on the disruptive student's shoulder, or even working the person's name or misbehavior into the story. For example, you might say, "The Little Red Hen always obeyed her mother, and she never poked at other students when she was listening to stories at Chicken School."

Often, if you ignore a person's disruptive behavior, it will stop. I recently conducted a workshop for a group of seniors, and two of them had a conversation in very audible voices while I was speaking. Others in the room looked annoyed, but none of them shushed the talkers. While I was trying to decide whether to say something, they subsided. I believe that if you speak up, you will always be cast as the villain by someone who observes you, no matter how tactful you try to be.

Of course, sometimes you may have to say something. I wait until the end of my story, and if possible say something quietly to the disruptive person, if I can do so without embarrassing or drawing attention to him or her, or to someone in charge.

Before you begin, look around the audience. Often you will be able to spot the troublemakers before they start. As the emcee is welcoming everyone, you may notice a few wiggleworms who are ignoring the speaker and wrestling or a few parents who have settled into the back of the group and are deep in conversation. You or the emcee can try to forestall disruptive behavior by explaining again that this is a listening space and that anyone who prefers to talk should go elsewhere to do so.

Olga Loya once found it effective to say, "Not yet," to two youngsters who were talking. They understood that they should wait to finish their conversation, and they quieted down.

When the Audience
Doesn't Respond

I once saw a famous performer get angry with an class of about 30 people because he didn't feel that they were living up to their part of the bargain that when a teller tells, the audience responds verbally and with body language that shows their interest. This particular audience was composed of extremely tired teachers who had put in a full day and then driven a long distance to attend the class. Some of them tried to perk up, but some of them pulled away mentally, put off by his anger. Perhaps if the performer had asked for help from the listeners, he might have gotten a better response than with a lecture on their responsibilities.

When Audience Members
Don't Participate

I never make an issue of listeners not participating in stories. Of course, I realize they may not be participating for any number of logical reasons: learning disabilities, shyness, hearing problems, lack of English, depression, and so on.

As we all know, children have different styles. Some will participate in an exuberant fashion, threatening to break your ear drums. Others may repeat the words occasionally or a beat behind everyone else or do only parts

of the gestures. I smile encouragingly at these students.

If you have a group that doesn't respond well to the participatory parts before the story begins, try a strategy of storyteller Joe Hayes: He starts the story and then asks the audience to help keep it going by participating. He finds that once people are involved and interested in the story, they are glad to repeat words and gestures.

When Listeners
Misunderstand the Story

Clarity

If you are mumbling or rushing through your words, your listeners won't be able to understand you. Give your listeners time to process what you are saying. This is particularly important if you are telling to non-native speakers of the language you are speaking. It's been estimated that one in seven students in California schools is not proficient in the English language.[1] If I know that many of my audience members don't know much English, I speak a little more deliberately.

If you are telling your story in a foreign (to you) language and have trouble pronouncing some words, say these words a little more slowly, with a tiny pause before and after, so the audience can understand you. Do the same if you are using words that may be unfamiliar to your audience, such as a character's name. For example, how many children have ever heard of the brave Japanese dog, whose story is told in many books, including *Folk and Fairy Tales from Around the World* by Ethna Sheehan? When you tell stories about Schippeitaro, say his name slowly the first time. Once the listeners have heard the word clearly, you can repeat it throughout the story at a more normal speed. Of course, you have to know how to pronounce the word yourself. Ask an expert.

Explanations

As you read or listen to a story you'd like to learn, ask yourself if there are any concepts or words you don't understand or that some listeners will want explained. If you can, find out more about the concepts and look up the words. I really appreciate the rare folktale book that has a pronunciation glossary, an introduction about the culture that explains unusual concepts, and lists of sources and recommended readings. Harold Courlander is one folklore collector whose books often do all this.

Decide if you're going to explain or define unusual words or concepts before, during, or after the story. Sometimes you might choose to use a word that your audience will already know, but I believe it's also important to widen listeners' vocabularies.

After the Story

When you've finished telling, let the story sink in for a moment. After a pause you can begin the introduction to the next tale or, if it's appropriate, ask if there are any questions or comments. You may be surprised at the misunderstandings some people have about your stories, but gently clear them up without letting others denigrate those who didn't "get it." I once had a listener think that when Molly Whuppie ran across a bridge of one hair, she was running over a "hare." After that, whenever I told the story, I would put up my hand in a gesture to show a thin strand of hair.

Sometimes after a story, I ask the children, "Did that really happen?" Together we shake our heads, "No." Then I ask, "Was it a story?" We nod our heads, "Yes."

I never say that it was "just a story" or that it wasn't true. I believe that there's no such thing as "just" a story and that there are important truths in fiction. Still, it is important for children to learn to tell the difference between reality and fantasy.

You can encourage adult listeners to ask the children later about what events in the story could or couldn't happen in the real world and to discuss the similarities and differences between fictional characters and people they actually know.

Speed

When you are telling to seniors and people who are hard-of-hearing, enunciate and slow down your pace. I try to imagine a little bubble around each word so that there are tiny pauses between each word. This makes understanding much easier for people whose mental processes may have slowed or who have trouble hearing. It meant a lot to me to have a woman at a senior's club comment, "This was the first program I've enjoyed in a long time because I could understand what you were saying, unlike those other speakers who talk too fast and mumble."

Accents and Dialects in Stories

Accents can be fun to play with during a telling, as long as they don't denigrate the cultural group they are meant to characterize. A southern teller told me that she doesn't mind "northerners" using a southern accent with each other, but she would wonder if we were making fun of her way of speaking if we used a southern dialect when telling to an audience in the South. When in doubt, ask permission of the audience or at least a member of the cultural group.

If you want to add accents to your repertoire, go to foreign films or check your local college library for dialect records. You can travel or talk to people you meet who have interesting accents.

Use accents as just that: an accent to add spice to the story. Rarely use a heavy accent or an unintelligible dialect, or you will lose the audience.

When Listeners React Inappropriately to Your Stories

Be aware of alternative meanings of words that could provoke gasps or sniggers. Some gangs are now using gestures very similar to American Sign Language. I innocently used the sign for the letter "F" in a program and heard a murmur run through a crowd of seventh-graders. Their teacher informed me that it's a gang sign, and that these days you're really only safe using sign language for very young children. The older ones know the other meaning.

When I told the tale "Drawing the Dragon" at a school for incarcerated young men, one Asian student seemed very interested. Anne Osborn, the librarian there, informed me that he had become a Buddhist and kept her busy finding pictures of dragons. She also said that this made the administration uncomfortable because dragons are sometimes used as gang symbols. She also pointed out that the blue of my dress was a gang color. If you are going to tell in an area infested with gangs, find out the gang signs, symbols, and colors to avoid.

There are certain archaic words that have acquired rude slang meanings. Decide how you will handle the inevitable snickers. If your ancient tales have cocks crowing, gay old times, riding on asses, fairies flitting, and faggots burning, it can be an opportunity to discuss the fact that words change over time and that the meanings of words should be taken in context.

I try to take great care in choosing my words, but I mentioned at a primary school that an elderly character was rich enough to have a maid and a butler. One of the kindergartners gasped aloud, "She said, 'Butt!' "

I also try to keep up on current events. In the past I have introduced folktales with judges in them by asking my listeners if they've ever watched Judge Wopner on "People's Court" and then remarking that he's not the only judge who's had silly people with crazy cases come before him. After the beginning of the O. J. Simpson trial, I couldn't use that introduction because when I tried it, I heard a lad say in an undertone, "Ito."

When There Are Other Reactions to Your Stories

You don't usually need to prepare for positive reactions, except for being gracious in response to people who sometimes gush after a show. You might feel that your show was good but not "outstanding," as they are blaring. Don't tell your fans how badly you think you did. It makes them feel that they must be fools for loving your performance. People who, however, disapprove of your stories will be covered in chapter 14.

What I'd really like to talk about in this section is other reactions.

I have told to hundreds of thousands of listeners, which includes more assemblies in elementary schools than I can count. I look at the 200–300 students and teachers who gather in front of me at a time, and sometimes one or two will stand out because they are obviously amused or because that one really "gets" the point of my tale. I will always remember the teacher who was so tickled by my telling of "Sody Sallyraytus" that she almost fell out of her chair laughing, and how I had to really concentrate to not let her gales of giggles throw my timing off. Still, I find it frustrating not to know the inner response behind all those faces.

One day I was at a school in Los Angeles County. After the assemblies I was spending the day visiting classrooms to conduct creative writing and student storytelling exercises. At lunch the principal told me that she had just spent two hours with a fifth-grade girl in her lap.

The child was affected by the true ghost story I had told about a mother who dies during a blizzard and comes back as a ghost to save her children. As the child left the auditorium, her teacher saw how upset she looked. She sent the girl to the principal who held her while she sobbed.

I felt guilty that I had scared the child. I mentally resolved to think twice before telling that story again.

But then the principal told me why the girl wept. The child had lost her mother to cancer two months before. For two months now the little girl had been feeling lonely and frightened. She could not sleep at night. She wanted to tell her father, but he had already taken her younger brother into his bedroom to sleep. She felt she could not burden him further, so she had shut her grief up inside herself until my story made her face her loss.

Now that a caring adult knew her secret, the school district counselor would be called in to talk to the student, and her father could be told to pay more attention to his brave daughter.

When I heard the principal's story, I knew why I had told that tale, and why I should keep on telling it. Sometimes stories have the power to heal in ways we aren't often lucky enough to find out about.

Stories of death and parents evoke strong reactions. After I told the same story at the Sierra Storytelling Festival, an older woman waited until everyone had left the room before telling me that she had seen the ghost of her mother several times and that she felt guilty for not thinking of her mother more often. I held her while she wept.

Know that your stories are not always just pleasant diversions, and be aware of the ones that might evoke strong reactions. Don't stop telling them—just be prepared.

Telling in Potentially Difficult Settings

Any setting can be perfect or a problem. I have told in schools where every child was a delight and in other schools where children were literally screaming or crying and were not removed. I have told outdoors under the partial shade of a sapling while a dog herded sheep almost into my area and told in the same setting the next year a few yards away where rapt audiences and I enjoyed the cool shade of a large, leafy tree.

Telling Outdoors

Having told outdoors at many folk festivals, Renaissance fairs, children's events, and shopping centers, I have learned through trial and error some pointers I would like to share.

1. Try to find a spot away from noisy activities (including being under an airport's flight path) but not so far off the beaten path that your potential audience can't find you.

2. Check the seating arrangements in advance.

    a. Will the sun be in your audience's eyes at any time of the day?

    b. Are chairs, hay bales, or grassy spots available to sit on?

    c. If your audience has to sit on a dusty or even a grassy area (which might become dew-covered or stain nice clothing), consider bringing carpets or blankets for people to share—or suggest your audience do so in your advance publicity.

3. Make a large, attractive sign that won't be blown over by the wind. Even if your contract specifies that the booker will provide such a sign, don't assume that they will remember this one detail among all the other things they have to plan. Your sign should clearly announce:

    a. Times (and dates if more than one) of telling

    b. Whether the stories are for children (preschool, primary, intermediate, or all ages), families, or adults

    c. Whether it is a free event, or the prices

    d. Who is telling (name of group or individuals)

    e. Subject of program, if there is one (for example: Ghost Stories)

4. If you are not a loud teller, arrange for a microphone—or quickly learn from a voice coach how to project.

5. Choose short, action-packed stories that are funny or scary (long, thoughtful stories are best for captive indoor audiences). Use audience participation and exaggerated gestures.

6. Decide whether to use other types of entertainment such as mime, song, music, puppets, or juggling as story stretchers and attention getters.

7. Be prepared for a mixed audience, probably leaning heavily towards small children, no matter what age you announced the stories were for.

8. If you audience is scant or nonexistent, go get 'em! One teller can start the program while other tellers walk around the nearby areas to invite people to come listen.

   a. Do so with a smile.

   b. Don't tell them you have little or no audience.

   c. Be sure to announce that it's a free program if it is.

   d. Hand out fliers about the program if you have them.

   e. Make announcements (live or pre-recorded) over the public address system several times before each show. "Storytelling by Ms. Blah-blah will begin in one half hour at the Shady Pavilion." This first announcement gives them time to get to the location where you will be performing if it is at a site that is large. Repeat the announcement 10 minutes before the show, five minutes before, and when it is time for the show to begin.

9. Bring sun block; a hat; lukewarm water; other noncaffeinated drinks; snacks; comfortable shoes; and clothes that are light-colored, don't too obviously show perspiration stains, and are made with at least 50 percent cotton.

Telling at Holiday Events

Holiday events can be chaotic, but if you have some idea of what to expect and how to prepare, you will be the calm center of the storm.

1. If it's a family or institution's (library, club, children's hospital, etc.) holiday party, expect the children to range in age from babies to teenagers.

   a. Be sure to ask the booker what ages the children will be.

   b. Be prepared for the age estimates to be wrong.

   c. Try to plan your longer stories to appeal to a wide age range, using very short stories, poems, songs, or finger plays to target specific age groups.

2. Ask if you can perform before the children eat. Otherwise they may be restless due to sugar and caffeine intake.

3. Ask to perform before Santa or the Easter Bunny arrives and insist that he keep completely out of sight until you are finished. (It's difficult to compete for attention with the real star and his gifts.)

4. Explain that storytelling needs a quiet setting. Don't let the booker put you next to the piano and carolers or on the main thoroughfare to the refreshment table.

5. When choosing stories, watch out for the overly sentimental ones especially prone to Christmas. The book may have gorgeous illustrations, but can the story stand alone?

6. If performing nonreligious tales in a public place, remember the Jewish children. Be sure to add one or more nonreligious Hanukkah or Passover tales to your program.

7. If you would like to do religious stories in a nonreligious setting, be sure to ask if it's all right beforehand.

8. Consider using stories already in your repertoire and giving them a holiday or seasonal setting. Of course, this won't work for every story but it can save you some story preparation. Why learn nonreligious Easter stories that can only be told once a year? Tell stories of Peter Rabbit, B'rer Rabbit, the White Rabbit of *Alice in Wonderland*, and other famous rabbits. Or tell folktales explaining how the rabbit got her long ears and short tail and why her nose always twitches. These tales turn up in many countries and

can be found in Margaret MacDonald's *Storyteller's Sourcebook*. Add as story stretchers your favorite finger plays about bunnies, and hand out origami rabbit's heads. These stories and stretchers can then be used separately in other programs, such as one on world folktales or "how and why" tales or animal stories.

Telling in Libraries

Many small libraries don't have a separate room for shows. If you are a storyteller who has only your voice with which to compete with noisy photocopy machines and drinking fountains, patrons who walk between you and the audience to get to the best-seller shelves, toddlers who don't understand the story and start talking, and so on, get to the library at least 30–40 minutes before the show and do what you can to minimize the distractions. I unplug the cord under electric water fountains if they are too near where I am telling. I try to persuade the librarian to put an out-of-order sign on the photocopying machine if I have to tell standing next to it. I try to put myself in an area where there are no visual distractions behind me and where I won't be in the path of well-used library materials.

Most libraries don't have enough staff to have someone stay during your entire show to handle crying babies, talking adults, vomiting children (yes, it happened, but thank goodness it was at the back of the group where only I and her mother seemed to notice), and other problems. In fact, I find it even helps to ask that the library staff lower their voices if I am within earshot of the checkout desk. Ask if a staff member can stay with you and handle any distractions in a quiet and tactful way. Have a friend help out, as I have had librarians just sit there while children ran and yelled during my show.

The greatest challenge facing America's libraries (and those of us who wish to perform in them) is a decreasing funding base. Join your local Friends of the Library group and help them raise money. Be sure to write letters to your politicians and to get out and vote

whenever library funding is at issue. I still give the libraries in my county the best deal in price because I value libraries and their services. Kent Cummins, a magician in Austin, Texas, charges nothing for library shows in his town because he feels he wouldn't be a magician today if as a child he had not been able to borrow books about magic from his local library.

Telling in Schools

Here's a scenario:

I walk into the school office and introduce myself to the secretary. She looks at me blankly and says, "Oh, are there assemblies today? Well, the multipurpose room is over there." She waves vaguely to the right.

I find the room and discover that it includes five black garbage cans surrounded by trash. I clean up the trash and move the cans. The custodian arrives to set up my mike just as the first class is filing in. He leaves before the shrill sound of feedback makes everyone clutch their ears. No one knows where he is or how to fix the mike.

I ask if everyone is here, and the teachers glance around and shrug their shoulders. I notice that there are fifth-graders sitting in the back of the room while the rest of the children are the first- and second-graders I was expecting. I ask the fifth-grade teacher why they aren't waiting for the intermediate assembly, and she says that she asked the principal if her group could come with the primary classes. I explain that I had not been told in advance of the change and that I had planned to tell stories appropriate to younger children, which the fifth-graders would consider babyish. I am frantically thinking of what stories I can do instead that will hit the middle ground of being simple enough for the little ones but mature enough for the older students. Now it is time to begin my show.

I would like to tell you that this set of circumstances happened only once and happened only to me, but every storyteller has had similar horror stories performing in schools and has learned to cope. I show up 30–60 minutes before my first show so I can clean up my space, test the mike, set up my portable sound system if necessary, and so on. I am then ready to welcome the first students as host of the story party they are going to be attending.

When you call the day before your show to make sure everything is on track, ask that the person in charge of setting up the system be reminded again of the time the equipment must be ready and of your requirements (such as a clip-on mike, etc.). If you need help unloading equipment from your car, ask that there be a person delegated to meet you in the office when you arrive.

Plan to introduce yourself at your assemblies, as most schools' staff are far too busy to act as emcees. If you prefer to be introduced, have a paper with a written introduction to give the emcee.

Scheduling Your Show

I still shudder a little bit when I remember telling to a group of Idaho high school students on the Friday afternoon before their two-week break to help their families harvest potatoes. Mentally, these students had already left on their vacation, and it showed in their lack of attention to my tales.

I am a morning person myself, so whenever possible, I schedule events for the morning. I also try to perform before audience members are to eat. People get sleepy and have trouble concentrating after meals because their blood has rushed to the stomach to aid in digestion.

Early evening is better than late evening. 7:00 P.M. as a starting time will generally draw more families of young children than 8:00 P.M., especially if it's a weeknight.

What you probably won't expect when scheduling your show is that it will be the same time that the city garbage handlers will be right outside your performance hall, banging giant dumpsters and backing up the truck with that annoying "beep, beep" warning signal, but trust me: it will happen eventually. Keep on smiling and talking.

What Else?

I'm sure that some zany, scary, or puzzling challenge will come up for you that I have not covered in this chapter or in other chapters. There is a Yiddish proverb that says, "God gave burdens, also shoulders." Why, a year after some huge mix-up occurs, you'll probably be using it as a funny story when dining out with your friends! Keep a sense of perspective, think quickly, and compliment yourself afterwards for surviving and perhaps even triumphing.

Resources

Further Reading

Courlander, Harold, and Wolf Leslau. *The Fire on the Mountain: And Other Stories from Ethiopia and Eritrea*. New York: Henry Holt, 1978.

———. *Terrapin's Pot of Sense*. New York: Holt, Rinehart and Winston, 1957.

———. *The Tiger's Whisker: And Other Tales from Asia and the Pacific*. New York: Henry Holt, 1987.

MacDonald, Margaret. *The Storyteller's Sourcebook: A Subject, Title, and Motif Index to Folklore Collections for Children*. Detroit: Gale, 1982.

Sheehan, Ethna. *Folk and Fairy Tales from Around the World*. New York: Dodd, 1970.

Notes

1. *BEOutreach Newsletter*, California State Department of Education Bilingual Education Office, January, 1990, 1.

Chapter 13

When It's Your Fault and Other Problems

Most of what I covered in the last chapter was challenges caused by others, but you can also be the source of the problem, sometimes through no real fault of your own.

Being Late; What a Week!

I had the most extraordinary run of good and bad luck one week in February 1993.

- **Bad Luck:** My car broke down in Walnut, California, more than 100 miles from home.
- **Good Luck:** It was on my way *from* not *to* my performance and 200 feet from the only phone available for a mile. I was quickly towed to a garage where I was able to reach the secretary at the school where I was to perform the next day and ask her for a ride from my hotel to the performance as it would take several hours for the mechanic to install a new timing belt.

- **Bad Luck:** A scant three days later on my way to Hesperia, a town more than 120 miles from home, the alternator died. It was at night on the highway.
- **Good Luck:** I was able to pull off the highway and walk to a nearby hotel to phone the American Automobile Association (AAA) again (!!) to tow me to a garage.

- **More Good Luck:** The garage was actually open at 5:30 p.m. on a Sunday and was able to replace my alternator within an hour.

- **Bad Luck:** The very next day I was on my way in a driving rain to a performance only to find the road to the school flooded and impassable.
- **Good Luck:** A kind person let me in to phone the school from his home so I could ask for an alternate route. I was able to arrive only five minutes late.

These incidents convinced me of two things: 1) that the money I spend on my automobile association membership with its free towing service and 800 roadside emergency phone number is worth every penny, and 2) that it was time to invest in a cellular phone. Any performer who travels a lot might find such investments worthwhile. Being stuck in rush-hour traffic, getting in a car accident, getting lost, or becoming suddenly ill—these are other reasons that might prevent you from getting to a gig on time. With a cellular phone, you can call the booker to let them know. They can give you directions or tell you if they are able to postpone, reschedule, or cancel your shows.

If anyone told you being a freelance performer in today's world was easy, worry-free, and inexpensive, then they have never had the week like the one that I survived. Oh, and I haven't told you what the two mechanics charged. . . .

Getting Lost

Another good thing about belonging to an automobile association is that they provide maps. Of course I always write the directions I receive into the contract so that if they are incorrect, it is the booker's fault, not mine. However, that's cold comfort when you discover after having gotten lost that the yellow house you were told to look for as a landmark had burned down the previous year. That's why I always try to arrive at a show at least 30 minutes in advance; it leaves a little time to get lost.

Forgetting a Show

Most performers don't like to even think about missing a show. It's a nightmare to be woken out of a sound sleep by a booker asking why you aren't on the stage at that very moment. It happened to me. My excuse is that the booking was made so far in advance that when I moved to my new house, the scheduling packet was lost—but there really is no excuse for 200 students waiting for a teller who doesn't show. I had to reschedule for another day, and I gave the school two copies of my book for their faculty lounge, a $50 rebate on my fee, and told the students that if they came to my Halloween show in a nearby park that Saturday, I would give each of them a sticker as a thank-you for being patient and understanding. You should decide exactly what you will do in similar circumstances.

I now write into my contract that the booker is to call me the day before my performances to tell me that everything is still on track for the next day. While it gives me a chance to make sure that last-minute changes haven't occurred, I really ask them to do it as a reminder.

Voice Problems

If your voice is too soft for listeners to hear easily, remember to take regular breaths, pick a listener at the back of the room to tell to, or use a small sound system with a microphone. Don't strain your voice trying to talk over a group that you've set loose to tell stories to each other. Instead use your sound system, or ring a bell to get their attention.

If you have problems with talking too low, losing your voice, or getting a sore throat when telling, I recommend reading *Freeing the Natural Voice* by Kristin Linklater. We all used to be able to cry for hours as babies or to talk loudly as toddlers. Ms. Linklater explains how to relax and to strengthen your vocal chords. If you are truly serious about being the best teller you can be, work with a local vocal coach. Find one through local theaters or college drama departments.

I protect my voice and throat by breathing deeply; drinking plenty of unchilled water between stories (iced water will freeze your throat); and doing relaxation, voice, and stretching exercises before telling. I always use a microphone with large groups.

Sickness

During a school year, I see thousands of children who can pass their illnesses on to me, so I get a flu shot every year and take plenty of vitamins. No matter how careful you are, though, sometimes you will just be too ill to perform and will have to cancel, reschedule, or even to cut short a show or workshop. Most people will be very understanding.

I once had the flu and tried to find a last-minute replacement to take over my Holiday Tales assembly (you can't reschedule Christmas vacation!). No one was available, so I took a thermos of hot tea laced with fresh lemon juice and honey and my bottle of cough medicine and drove to the school. Of course their sound system went out so that despite my sore throat I had to project to a large room filled with students. Somehow I managed, but I don't recommend trying to go on if you really are too ill.

Nervousness, Anger, Depression, Physical Discomfort

Imagine that you have just had your home magically cleaned for the best party you've ever given. Friends and family are beginning to arrive. A few of them are a little shy. It is up to you to make them feel welcome. That's how I see myself as a storyteller. When I stand up to begin my program, I am inviting my listeners into my home: the story space. I want them to feel relaxed, happy, and an integral part of the group. I put aside any physical, mental, or emotional discomfort I am feeling to concentrate on having a wonderful story party.

At the end of the party as people leave with smiles and thanks, I often find that any discomfort I felt earlier has been replaced by a warm glow of satisfaction.

Preventing and Coping with Storyteller Burnout

After telling stories for seven years, I wrote the following in my May 1987 newsletter:

Help! When I first started to tell, I was excited about learning how to explore my talent and challenged by trying to make a living from an unusual art form. Schools proved to be my main source of bookings. I found that I was spending a good part of my time giving one or two prepared lectures on storytelling in classrooms or performing in assemblies. I arrive at a school, check in at the office, speak to a small or large sea of young faces, exchange a few words with a teacher or two, and go home to my office where I work alone on correspondence and writing.

Slowly I've become aware of what a lonely, unfulfilling life this is. The listeners gain in individual, private ways from the stories. They may stop for a moment to tell me that they liked my tales, but since I'll probably never see them again, I don't know what dreams or changing memories or insights they'll have from what they heard. I form no real relationships with them. I no longer find myself fed by their shining faces.

The intellectual stimulation is no longer there, either. I gain little information I didn't already have from reading the same story plots served up in yet another version in folklore collections or from reading one of the 27 storytelling newsletters to which I subscribe. The act of telling even my favorite stories has become old hat.

Storytelling is still my career of choice, but I need advice. Everyone in every job experiences burnout at some time. What I want to know is how do you or would you handle any aspect of storyteller burnout. All suggestions will be gratefully received.

Twelve wonderful storytellers from around North America sent in useful ideas, and I've reprinted their suggestions here. Again I send them my heartfelt thanks for caring enough to respond to my plea. I would add to all their excellent suggestions that it is important to find people who support you in what you do and to stay away from naysayers whose negativity can sap your enthusiasm. When your friends and family try to discourage you from such a foolhardy venture as being a freelance storyteller, listen politely. Explain how much it means to you. Tell them your game plan so they won't think you've jumped off the deep end without a net. Ask them to help. Can they research a low-cost health insurance plan for you, pay part of your car loan, recommend you as a teller to a club or church they belong to, show up at a public performance to cheer you on, pass out fliers at their place of work? Be sure to find a support group or special friend to talk to when times are tough mentally, financially, or emotionally.

The Voices of Experience: Twelve Tellers Provide Advice

Burnout, ah yes, a problem in any field but perhaps especially so in the arts where so much of our work is a lonely struggle without the recognition our culture considers big-time success.

Cathryn Wellner, Canada

Poor Harlynne. Your newsletter which always seems personally addressed to me has done so much to alleviate my isolation. But unless you're getting much feedback it's no wonder you're feeling drained. The loneliness of the long distance editor is a problem in itself.

Fran Stallings, Oklahoma

1. Stop and think.

One of the questions I find it profitable to ask myself when stress rears its formidable head is: "What is it about the path I'm now following that is making me so tired, depressed, etc., and what awaits me at the end of the path if I don't change something now?"

Michael Parent, Virginia

2. Be aware of yourself as inspiration.

When I was at the Child Research Center in Washington, D.C., as a student (three years old), a magician storyteller came and performed. I think of how I remember that magician some 40 plus years later and say to myself, "Maybe that girl in the third row will remember this story—I better make it good. . . ."

Caroline Feller Bauer, Florida

I was inspired by a performer who came to my school when I was 15; he sowed the seed of an idea in me that eventually became a career for me. And I feel if I can be that same spark of an idea for anyone else, then I have been a success. I have another attitude in my shows. I am offering something of real value. I am trying to tell kids some valuable stuff that I wish I had known at their age. I have various messages, like "read books!" Maybe you could be a crusader against TV. Maybe you are already! I feel that you must believe in what you are doing.

Paul Tracey, California

Most of these kids who you visit and tell to will never again experience true storytellers of your quality. In just giving these children that lone exposure, you are doing something unique, something special for their lives. Perhaps, one or two will find that delight, test themselves, become inspired to tell or act or come out of his or her shell and blossom. Like the forester we've planted the seeds—special seeds—in hopefully fertile soil. The tree takes time to grow, and seldom does that seed-planter see the results. Maybe it's enough to know we've been given the talent and energy to plant the seeds well. Some of the trees will be very special. We need to remember this. (Wow! Is this vine replacement!)

Robert Rubinstein, Oregon

3. Do something different.

Storytelling is very much a verbal, head-and-heart activity. When I'm exhausted with words and feelings, a non-verbal or physical activity can be an antidote. Maybe large muscle things (dig the garden, swim laps, move furniture). Maybe visual-creative things (draw, paint, take photos). Maybe auditory things (make or listen to music). Storytelling is immaterial: we're left with nothing to see/touch after all that effort. My favorite professor did woodworking to counter the frustration of seldom seeing what became of her students.

Fran Stallings, Oklahoma

Have a baby! Then you'll no longer experience storyteller burnout—you'll enjoy *total burnout*! Seriously, what I mean is to recheck one's *total life*—the balance in it! When I find myself worried about storytelling or feeling "ruttish," I change activities for awhile—usually doing something very concrete—for example, housecleaning (ugh—but a freshly washed and even—perhaps—waxed floor—WOW!)

Cathy Spagnoli, Washington

4. Take care of yourself.

I suspect that the real source of and solution to the burnout may have been what was going on in the other areas of your life. When I'm getting plenty of sleep, getting plenty of vitamins, and getting along with my husband and children, I find that I'm much more satisfied with my professional life too.

Betty Ann Wylie, Georgia

Basic health, strength, energy are of the utmost importance.

Paul Tracey, California

Spend some time every day being good to yourself. A quiet moment of meditation, or planting something in the garden, or whatever. It sounds like you are a real on-the-go person, putting out, putting out all the time. Some nurturing seems in order.

Nan Gregory, British Columbia

My antidote is space and time. A few days by the ocean or under the endless sky of the intermountain west, and my soul is restored. But time, too, for lunch with a friend, an evening at the theatre, a morning with a good book, an hour with my journal. These are sources of renewal for me.

Cathryn Wellner, Canada

Keep and nurture a sense of humor.

Cathy Spagnoli, Washington

Come here and sit on my front porch and drink a gin and tonic—anytime; I mean it.

Nan Gregory, British Columbia

5. Pace yourself.

Remember that you don't have to accept every offer that comes in over the phone and to block out times on your calendar when you flat out will not do engagements. This will allow you to be receptive, to let things in.

Michael Parent, Virginia

6. Try something new.

Expand your skills. Study singing, clog dancing, origami, signing for the deaf— anything that might push your limits of storytelling. Explore the other arts. Go to galleries, plays, jazz concerts, new music festivals, and let the genius and aspirations of others feed you.

Nan Gregory, British Columbia

I do sometimes get tired of even favorite stories and just rotate them out of my repertoire for awhile till I want to tell them again. I think new props, new costumes, new characters, new stories, new magic tricks, helped at times.

Betty Ann Wylie, Georgia

You could consider changing the direction and themes of your stories.

Lloyd Brennecke, Illinois

Do anything except what you know you can comfortably do. Stop the old stuff, and sometimes new will appear. The truth is, of course, that boredom comes not from what you do, but from your attitude toward what you do. To overcome boredom you must shake up your attitudes, and that means do something that scares you, that challenges you, that is risky for you, something that really forces you (your deep dark inner you) out onto the line.

Kendall Haven, California

Keep your storytelling work varied— seek new challenges. For me, that means finding various different audiences so that my repertoire can grow in many ways and my telling style as well. Collaborating with other artists was extremely energizing and gave us all many new ideas. A program for toddlers (for my diaper service) resulted in a fun week of stitching "Super Diaper" out of 12 diapers and then making up exploits to share. Work in prison made me find more varied stories for women, including those on abuse and gay women. A commission for the Museum of Flight here has me creating a space fantasy.

Cathy Spagnoli, Washington

7. Continuity is important.

Have you ever tried a residency at a school where you go several times and build up students' storytelling abilities? This way you would have to get a good idea of the effect you are having.

Paul Tracey, California

What has worked for me is to find some way that I can develop an ongoing relationship with one group that I meet with for an hour a week. In your case this might be financed by developing a grant proposal that pays you to do something such as "develop listening skills, attention span, vocabulary, self-image . . . " through using folktales with children. Sustained contact means one can develop a thread—tell a number of stories on a theme, use the same story with several evolving follow-ups, and see the children grow and mature.

Anonymous

"Adopt" a neighborhood school, Sunday school class, pediatric hospital ward, Scout troop, etc. Repeated visits with a specific group will develop a sense of community. Isolation can lead to burnout, although there's a certain interest and excitement in being with different people every day.

Betty Ann Wylie, Georgia

Volunteer to tell stories on an ongoing basis at, say, a hospital for sick children or a home for the aged. Return visits would mean that the faces lighting up at your approach would be ones you know, and you would know, too, that you meant more to them than an hour's pastime.

Nan Gregory, British Columbia

My second antidote is teaching adults. Whenever my spirits flag, and I begin to doubt the importance of the work, a new group of students discovering storytelling's power for the first time re-ignites my own fire.

Cathryn Wellner, Canada

8. Find fellow tellers/performers.

My best antidote is getting involved with other storytellers. We are fortunate here in Seattle to have a large and active Guild and a core of professional tellers who appreciate the need for interaction. I find being an active part of NAPPS (National Association for the Preservation and Perpetuation of Storytelling—now the National Storytelling Association) is essential to keeping me artistically alive. Being part of a network of storytellers around the country keeps me stretching and exploring the art.

Cathryn Wellner, Canada

A peer group helps a lot, unless it's part of the problem—as a group that leans on you for leadership would be.

Fran Stallings, Oklahoma

Try working with a partner. Choose a theme or set a project, and work with someone else for a bit. Although it has its difficulties—Lord knows!—working with my partner is inspiring, fun, and it's very nice to have a companion to chat with when times get low. So you could choose as your partner for this project: another storyteller or a musician or an artist or an expert in children's games. Anyone who can help you expand your idea of how to tell.

Nan Gregory, British Columbia

9. Change professions.

When you hold a children's librarian position in a good public library, you not only tell stories almost daily, but you see the children's growth from them. You see children go from age two at the toddler story time, when they can barely concentrate on one story, to very story-sophisticated five-year-olds who can really carry on a conversation with you about what stories they like and why, and who can sit still responsively for your favorite 45-minute story. You get to see all the best story books as soon as they come

in and have first choice of new books to learn, or to recommend to your listeners as an extension of what you've told. The children become your fans and friends and network for you among their siblings and friends and adults.

Anne Osborn, California

10. Etc.

I get letters from the kids afterwards, and this gives me a pretty good idea of the effect I have had on them. I always use their letters as my writing paper, writing (on the back side) because I like to spread the joy that I find in their writing.

Paul Tracey, California

I find the cultural research behind storytelling fascinating and even renewing. Following my own needs, with an Indian husband, a mixed-race child, and six years in Asia finished and more to come, I try to spend time reading, studying, and writing particularly about Asian oral literature (so much more than just folk tales). I like to spend time as well collecting stories from people of this background—not just relying on books.

Cathy Spagnoli, Washington

Doing eight performances a week, people ask, "How do you keep it so fresh?" Every audience is a new one, and we had to pound every audience into submission! We had to win over each audience; it was not good enough to rely on a good review in the paper. It made no difference how good you were last night. And so I accepted each night as a challenge.

Paul Tracey, California

Resources

Further Reading

Linklater, Kristin. *Freeing the Natural Voice.* New York: Drama Book Specialists, 1976.

Chapter 14

Only You Can Answer
Questions About Prejudice, Fear, Censorship, and Stories

The Miller, His Son, and Their Donkey:
An Aesop's Fable Retold

One day a miller and his son decided to take their donkey to town to sell at the market. As they walked down the road, the donkey trudging along behind, the father began to get tired. "Son, I'm going to ride the donkey for awhile," he said, climbing onto the animal's back.

A little farther down the road, they passed some women carrying eggs to market. One of them said to another in a loud whisper, "Do you see that? The poor child must walk while the adult takes his leisure by riding the donkey!" The miller overheard and felt so badly that he insisted his son take his place.

Farther along they came upon a farmer leading a cow to market. "What are you doing, lad? You are young and strong, and yet you make your old father walk in this heat!"

"He is right, Father. Perhaps you should join me on the donkey." The miller clambered on board. The two began singing to pass the time.

Their song was interrupted by a fine lady in a carriage. "Disgraceful! That small animal forced to carry two large humans. Get off at once!" They hastened to obey and stood looking at each other in dismay as the carriage drove off.

"The only thing left to do, Son, is to reward our poor donkey by carrying him awhile," suggested the miller. Somehow they hoisted the beast onto their shoulders, but as they staggered across the bridge into the town, they fell, dropping the animal into the river where it drowned.

MORAL: When storytellers try to please all listeners, they lose the story.

The End 📖

Why Do You Tell Stories?

If your answer is, "I tell stories only to make a buck," then don't bother to read the rest of this chapter. Just remember the French proverb, "Money is a good servant but a bad master." Don't let money make you forget your art and your morals.

Maybe you replied, "I tell stories to serve as a bridge between cultures." Perhaps you see your stories as a way to show your listeners that people laugh and cry for the same reasons all over the world and that the listeners' prejudices are ridiculous. In 1988, the National Congress on Storytelling was held in Santa Fe, New Mexico. The purpose of the congress was to discuss methods of presenting stories from different cultural traditions in a way that created respect and awareness.

Steve Sanfield, California poet and author, suggested that believing you can be a bridge between cultures might be a pompous attitude. Jon Spelman, Washington, D.C. actor and storyteller, asked that you confront your own prejudices first and to help fight racism in yourself and in others. One way to do this, according to Len Cabral of Rhode Island, is to "change the world one child at a time."

Peninnah Schram explained, "In Jewish tradition each person has three names: the name that is given at birth, the name given by others, and the name each person gives him or herself. If you give yourself the name 'Story-teller,' you must live up to that special name because that name carries such responsibility."

What Is a Storyteller?

One Native American at the Congress complained that when professional performers come to her area and are called "storytellers," the children decide that if the professional's dramatic renditions on the stage are storytelling, then their own parents and others in their community who have shared narratives with them in a low-key way are not storytellers.

Len Cabral suggested that you have children tape their parents telling stories in their first language, which the students then translate for the rest of the class. Then they will understand that their families are full of storytellers and to be proud of their first language.

Where Do You Belong as a Storyteller?

If a school calls and asks you, a white teller, the only storyteller they know, to do a program in honor of Black History Month, do you have a responsibility to recommend an African American performer instead? Of course, keep in mind that not all tellers from a particular race want to be pigeon-holed in that way. They may wish more bookers would hire them on the strength of their abilities rather than just because of their color.

If you wish to find "folk" tellers to re-place you in certain situations, go to tiny ethnic festivals. They won't be on the stage necessarily, but sitting on a folding chair hold-ing court. If they agree to tell in a situation outside of their community, they may feel more comfortable telling in a small room to a small group rather than using a microphone on a stage before a large audience.

Who Do You Ask for Permission to Tell?

At another conference also sponsored by the National Storytelling Association, an Afri-can American librarian was asked by a white woman whether it was all right for white tellers to tell African American stories. She replied, "I tell white stories, and is that all right? You go right ahead and tell black stories!"

Of course, no one person from any par-ticular culture can speak for all members of that culture. Other African Americans may be offended by any white person using an African or African American story. Some people will be angry if you tell other cultures' stories for any reason.

How Do I Show Respect to Other Storytellers?

There has been a trend in storytelling toward telling personal experience stories rather than folktales. Part of the reason is that narratives about your life are a little harder for others to take and tell (though it does happen). I use the true account of how I broke my leg the day before I started seventh grade to model for students the art of shaping a memory into a story. At one school a girl insisted that she had heard the story—but not from me. I assume that a teacher had heard me tell the story and was now using my story rather than coming up with a memory of her own.

Others who share shattering personal experiences or who create "signature" stories from researching and adapting oral narratives are far more upset when they find someone else telling them as their own. Olga Loya had this happen to her when her version of "La Cucarachita" ("The Little Cockroach") was being told by someone in another state. The other performer was told in no uncertain terms that she was violating Olga's copyright and never to do it again.

This issue was brought up at our 1993 retreat, and we wrote the following Storytelling Etiquette Statement to educate amateur and freelance professionals about their responsibilities to their colleagues. We urge you to copy the statement and read it or pass it out at storytelling events.

Storytelling Etiquette Statement

This Storytelling Etiquette statement was compiled by Barbara Griffin, Olga Loya, Sandra MacLees, Nancy Schimmel, Kathleen Zundell, and Harlynne Geisler. Please pass it out or read it at storytelling events.

Stories are to share and tell. While we encourage the art of sharing stories, we want to encourage respect in our community.

You deserve respect. Respect other tellers.

A storyteller's personal, family, and original stories are her or his copyrighted property. It is unethical and illegal to tell another person's original, personal, and family stories without the permission of the author or storyteller.

Folklore and folktales are owned by the public, but a specific version told by an individual teller or found in a collection is the author's or teller's copyrighted property. If you like a folktale a storyteller has told, ask that teller for a reference or where it can be found. Research the story by finding other versions, and then tell it your way.

Published literary tales and poetry are copyrighted material. They may be told at informal story swaps, but when you tell another's story in a paid professional setting, you need to request the permission of the publisher or author. Research copyright law.

When telling anywhere, it is common courtesy to credit the source of your story.

Pass stories, share stories, and encourage respect within the storytelling community.

How Do Your Stories Portray Other Cultures?

At an evening concert at the National Congress on Storytelling in Santa Fe, two Anglo tellers told Hispanic stories. One story was of a Mexican man who was so lazy that he stole all of his food from others and only exerted himself not to get caught. The other tale was of a Chicano trickster who had to sneak into heaven, where he stole God's liquor and angel feathers. Neither performer intended to say through their choice of tales that all Latinos are liars and thieves. After all, every culture has tales of fools and of tricksters. Yet because both stories were full of negative characteristics and were told by people outside the ethnic group, Hispanics within the audience were offended.

I tell a story I've adapted from a Mexican American tale about a man who is so stupid that he is sure to betray a fact best kept secret. I changed the character to one who is so honest that he can only tell the truth. The rest of the plot remains the same, but, oh, what a difference in how the character is perceived!

Don't speak of Native Americans and their stories in the past tense. These cultures and their stories are very much alive. Watch for romanticizing other cultures. Don't pass on negative stereotypes.

Look at your repertoire. Do your stories from other cultures present only characters who are stereotypes? Are all Hispanic characters presented as poor rural farmers, Native Americans as noble savages, and so on? If you are hesitant about a particular tale, ask people from the story's culture how it sounds to them. Get more than one opinion, as no one person can speak for an entire group.

How do you present these stories? Do you use a heavy accent that makes the characters speak foolishly? Do you give any background information to introduce the story and set it within a cultural context?

Researching Stories from Other Cultures

Some people will insist that you understand why a tale is told in a particular culture, how to pronounce any unusual words, and the meaning of all aspects of the tale as it relates to the culture. Cathy Spagnoli is a teller of Asian stories who has been to India and Japan several times in search of stories and tellers. Because not all tellers have unlimited time for cultural research, she recommends finding a culture you already know—by birth or interest—or one you are drawn to. Then you won't mind spending some time learning more about it. Once you have a base in one culture, you can work on several stories from the area to make the research "stretch." Then the next step would be a neighboring culture. This is the way she's been extending her knowledge of Asian stories.

Consider talking to the proprietors of a local ethnic restaurant in the hopes of meeting someone knowledgeable in the folklore and history of that culture. Also be aware of the culture's manner of speaking with others; for example, Native American and Chinese cultures are less direct than white culture.

Do not assume that every person from another culture will be thrilled about the idea that you wish to tell stories of that group. Peter Garcia, Hopi Indian and Chicano, made a moving plea to Anglo storytellers saying, "You've stolen everything from the Indians. Do you have to take our language too? Let us talk for ourselves. If exploitation is going to be done, let us do it ourselves. We don't want our culture to be trivialized. If you grew up on this earth, you have a culture. Tell us about your culture."

For more information on telling stories in different cultures, read the books and articles recommended in the "Resources" section at the end of this chapter.

Adapting Folktales

You will notice that the title of this section assumes folktales will be adapted. Every tale has been changed, whether by the generations that handed it down by word of mouth or by the folklorists who tidied it up to make it more appropriate to their audiences, by the translators (who changed Cinderella's fur slipper into the more famous glass one in a mistranslation), by the writers who put "retold" or "adapted" on their title pages, or by the performers who present it in a fashion that might be dramatically different from how it was originally told. No one can in all honesty read a translation of a Zulu tale in a children's collection at an American library, tell it to the children there, and believe that the telling is a genuine re-creation of the original story as told by Africans.

So the question is, How much can you change a tale without violating the integrity of the story? If a person from that background was in your audience, would he or she be angered or bewildered by what you've done to the story?

The most important guideline that I can give you is advice from Olga Loya: "Read many different stories from that same culture. This will give you a better sense of what is integral to the tale you've chosen." Olga also recommends that you be aware of who your audience is going to be. For example, there are many stories about death in the Mexican culture. These stories sometimes seem harsh to people outside of that culture. Olga likes to tell stories about "La Llorona," the weeping ghost of a woman who murdered her children. She tells these tales to young Spanish-speaking children because they are familiar with story, but she doesn't tell them to English-speaking youngsters who would find them too frightening. She is disturbed by tellers who try to make Mexican stories kinder and gentler.

Another instance of tellers changing a story to meet American sensibilities is a Vietnamese legend of a woman whose husband unjustly accuses her of infidelity. She commits suicide by walking into the river. The husband then discovers his mistake. The tale is well known by Vietnamese of all ages. I heard Cathy Spagnoli, a Seattle storyteller who has worked with the Asian immigrants in her city, tell the story.

Later, I found the story retold as "The Shadow on the Wall" in the children's book *The Beggar in the Blanket and Other Vietnamese Tales* by Gail Graham. This California author spent three months in Vietnam and had read several books of Vietnamese folklore written in French. She changes the ending (or perhaps the French author of the book she found it in changes it—hard to tell as she doesn't credit her sources) to the wife wandering away distraught and returning to overhear her husband discovering he is wrong about her infidelity. She forgives him, and they live happily ever after.

There seems to be a trend toward changing all tales for children to have happy endings, leading to the erroneous impressions that only bad people suffer. If you would like to read a more authentic version of this tale, look at "The Lady of Nam Xuong" in *Beyond the East Wind: Legends and Folktales of Vietnam* by Van Quyen Duong and Jewell Reinhart Coburn. Ms. Coburn has used a version sent to her by Van Quyen Duong in a letter from Vietnam.

When the question of violence in fairy tales arises at workshops I am conducting, I always remind people that there is often an excellent reason for that action within the story. The action may be symbolic. If the teller is offended by the violence, I suggest that they find another story to tell, rather than changing the original. Remember, though almost all folktales have now been relegated to the kiddie room, many of them, such as the Grimm fairy tales, were not originally intended for children.

Stereotypes of
Women and Men in Stories

Most storytellers, if not active feminists, will agree that female characters should be shown to play a wider spectrum of roles in stories than they have been traditionally. Without discarding fairy tales whose major characters are passive girls and evil women, most tellers have tried to add stories that show women as brave, intelligent, strong, active people interested in more than husbands, children, and housework. These tellers might even have prepared a program titled, "She-roes or Women of the World," or have been part of such a show.

This is the 1990s, after all—a time when children and adults should become aware of all the options available to them. Stories can help us shape our lives because we identify with the characters. Why else would Whoopi Goldberg refer to herself as Cinderella with a size 9 shoe or Sally Field call her life a repeat of the Little Red Hen fable?

Most storytellers try to teach as well as entertain with their narratives. They choose tales that talk of the evil of war and violence, the equality of all people, and the dignity of the elderly. Sometimes the lessons are stated outright. Sometimes they are subtle messages within the narratives.

Look at your entire repertoire of stories. How many have female animals or people as main characters? How many have females portrayed in positive ways? How many have males shown as sensitive, willing to expose their emotions, caring for children and homes, or learning that violence is not the answer? You may be surprised to find that women and men are depicted in the usual stereotypical ways most of the time. In fact, you may find that 75 percent or more of your narratives focus on males with females playing peripheral parts.

Because so many of us take pride in relating myths, legends, and folktales of the past, we help to continue the attitudes of the past. Look again at your male-dominated stories. Without doing violence to the spirit of the tale, can you change a male character to a female? Why not make the denigrating mother in "Jack and the Beanstalk" into a father? The Brothers Grimm had no qualms about changing evil fathers in some of their collected stories into evil stepmothers in later editions of their book.

Of course, you might prefer to change lesser-known tales instead, or to discuss the attitudes with your listeners before or after telling the tale "straight."

Should I Tell Traditional Tales
About Evil Stepmothers?

Child psychologist Bruno Bettelheim suggested that the reason so many fairy tales start with a loving mother dying and an evil stepmother taking over is so that the child who hears the tale can safely deal with anger at his or her own parent. Because children are not allowed to express hatred towards their mothers, the tales split the mother into two parts. One part loves the child unconditionally. The other part may be abusive or even— horror of horrors!— force the child to do such things as cooking and cleaning. That evil part may even seem to love other siblings better.

Roger Sale had a different explanation for evil stepmothers in his book *Fairy Tales and After: From Snow White to E. B. White*. He writes that the time period of most fairy tales was one of high mortality for women, especially during childbirth. It was a fact of life that men often remarried and that a second wife might resent children from a previous marriage who would inherit more because of their place in the birth order.

Nowadays stepmothers are once more a fact of life because of the high divorce rate. I am curious as to whether children are disturbed by the dark portrait of stepmothers in the old stories. (I have already found that some stepmothers are uneasy about being described as vengeful witches in fairy tales.) Does it help to prepare the children before telling the story by talking about real stepmothers and how loving they can be and by explaining that this is just a story? Or should we think twice before including evil stepmother stories in our repertoire?

Some feminists would prefer that such tales were forgotten because such stepmothers as the evil queen in Snow White are in conflict with younger women considered more beautiful because of their youth. Such tales are not a good example of sisters united against chauvinistic views of what makes a woman attractive. However, each storyteller has to decide as an individual and a professional how to handle evil stepmother stories. Be sure to consider all viewpoints before making up your mind.

When Someone Complains

How do I handle complaints about my stories?

I am Sir Oracle,
And when I open my lips let no dogs bark!
    —Merchant of Venice, 1, i, 93

To tell a story is to take a risk. Oh, it's not just the risk of standing in front of a group and speaking (the number-one fear of the average American, ranking above fear of death). No, the risk I'm talking about is that of taking a stand. Let's say you decide to tell a simple fairy tale such as Little Red Riding Hood. Where could the conflict be? Why, Charles Dickens himself said, "Little Red Riding Hood was my first love. I felt that if I could have married Little Red Riding Hood, I should have known perfect bliss." What could be nicer?

Are you going to tell the version where the wolf puts Grandma in the closet and is frightened away by the woodcutter before he can eat Little Red? Folklorists will protest this watering down of the original folktale.

Perhaps you'll choose an earlier version. In Charles Perrault's version, "Le Petit Chaperon Rouge," Little Red is eaten by the wolf to show children what will happen if they talk to strangers and stray from the path. (Charles Perrault is best known for creating in 1697 the version of Cinderella which most of us know today.) If you tell that story, you will very likely get objections for the extreme nature of the lesson.

The Grimm Brothers' "Little Red-Cap" might catch your fancy. Both Grandma and Little Red are swallowed by the wolf, but the woodcutter rescues them by cutting the wolf open with a pair of scissors. They then fill the wolf's body with stones. When he tries to run away, he falls down dead. Many feminists will hate the story as yet another sexist example of males endangering and rescuing helpless females. You could reduce that problem somewhat by telling the little-known incident included at the end of the Grimm Brothers story. When a second wolf tries to fool Little Red, she's too smart. Her grandmother has her fill a great stone trough with water in which they have boiled sausages. The wolf, who has climbed up on Grandma's roof, smells the sausage water and leans so far out that he ends up falling off the roof and into the trough, where he drowns.

But none of these stories will sit well with animal rights activists who will ask why you must continue to pick on the poor harmless wolf.

If you tell the story as the Grimm Brothers wrote it, people concerned about alcohol abuse will ask you to change the fact that Little Red is taking wine to a sick older lady. You may have read of the furor created by Trina Schart Hyman's picture book version of the tale which shows Grandma (portrayed with a red nose) actually drinking the wine at the end of the story, just as she does in the narrative collected by the Grimms. Still, you could explain before beginning the tale that most Germans do not view moderate wine drinking as evil, and that the story dates back in time to a period when water was unsafe so everyone drank wine.

If you tell Charles Perrault's version translated into English, be prepared for some snickers and gasps when you mention the faggot-makers in the forest. Even young children seem to know the contemporary meaning of the words, so again, a brief explanation may be in order before your telling. You can explain that *faggot-makers* is the archaic term for woodcutters.

A few extreme fundamentalists will object to any story that has talking animals in it as smacking of magic, another word that to them is synonymous with Satanism.

Some parents will protest that the violence of a wolf threatening to eat a helpless child might give their wee ones bad dreams.

In other words, just opening your mouth can cause problems—but then you're a talker (or you wouldn't be considering storytelling as a career), and you already know that.

You may receive complaints about any tale from people with political, religious, cultural, and parental concerns. Decide whether a story suits both you and your intended audience and which version rings the truest to you. If you feel that a story will be wrong for a particular group or that a few listeners might object, you must make the hard decision on how to respect the story's integrity, yourself as an artist, and your audience members' right to their beliefs. If you are asked to change a story radically to suit a booker, you may prefer to tell a different story or to turn down the booking.

Objections:
One Experience

In October 1993, I was asked to tell spooky stories at a school two days before Halloween. I barely made it to the school before my car died, the brakes smoking. I should have seen the problems that occurred coming, but can only offer my fear of being stranded in a city 100 miles away from home to explain why my antennae weren't up.

First, I'd been told by the PTA mother not to mention the "H" word (Halloween), because the week's theme was "Fall into Reading," ending with a parade of students dressed as literary characters. Right then and there I should have said that it might be better if I did multicultural folktales instead, but I love spooky stories. So I readily agreed to the woman's conditions and assured her that I'd tell spooky stories that could be found in children's books available in most school and public libraries.

My next warning came when she mentioned to me shortly before my first assembly that one student had wanted to dress as the witch from *The Wizard of Oz*, but had been discouraged. When I indignantly asked if the child was being prevented from doing so by anyone other than her parents, she gave me an evasive answer.

My third warning was when before another assembly the woman anxiously asked if my stories were going to be scary. I blithely assured her that they weren't.

As I told my three stories, I had all the students' rapt attention. None of the 250 children in my audience was covering their eyes or ears or biting their fingers (signs of fear to watch for), though many had very wide eyes fixed on me. In addition, the tales were all ones that I considered child-tested. I'd told them in many shows and often had children remark on how much they liked them. In 13 years only one Christian parent had ever objected to one of the tales. And she did so gently.

This day the teachers didn't seem to be with me. I ended with a funny story about the bogeyman. The usual crowd of kids gathered around me to ask to see my string figures again.

After they left, the PTA mother came up and told me that she and the teachers were upset at the violence in my tales, and that her daughter and others were going to have nightmares. I tried to tell her that the children should all be told again that my tales were fiction and suggested that they tell frightened children that putting their shoes in opposite directions under their beds would keep monsters away. She refused to say anything to the students about such charms, saying it just encouraged them to believe in unreal things. I was further reprimanded for saying in one of my tales that holy water kept evil away—no religion allowed in the schools, you know. I asked the woman to please let me know if any children reported nightmares, or if any parents or teachers had any other objections. She departed in a huff.

Then the custodian approached me. "I listened to your stories, and as a parent I found nothing to object to in them. I think that you ought to know that lady doesn't let her daughter watch anything but Disney—no news programs or anything else."

I thanked the custodian and went out to wait for the auto club to tow my car to a mechanic. While I sat there, I made up my list of options. They included:

1. To never tell spooky stories of any kind in schools again (I was very upset).

2. To never tell in assemblies again (very, very upset).

3. To send copies of stories to the principal in advance to okay (out of my mind).

4. To lay low for five years and see if this wave of censorship dies away (though I know rationally that if we artists all run scared, the censors will grow stronger).

5. To be like storyteller Steve Sanfield and be glad that I've stirred things up and made people think.

6. To realize like storyteller Pleasant DeSpain that 10 percent of people are not going to like what you do, no matter what it is.

7. To listen carefully to what people are saying they really want.

I never received a letter from the woman who objected to my scary stories, but I do worry that she is busy telling other schools never to hire me. I found it affecting my performances ever since. Now when I tell spooky stories (and I like to end my intermediate-age assemblies with one—most students' favorite type of story), I find myself watching the adults anxiously to see if they approve and wondering if any children that leave the room do so because their religion forbids them from listening to such tales. It was months later before I told those three stories again. I think I was affected not only by the many times I have been told at schools not to mention anything supernatural but also by the many cases of problems that I have heard from other tellers around the country.

I have told stories in a school where the principal has taken every book that has the word *witch* mentioned in it—even cute little picture books—off the shelves of the library without asking for anyone's consent. However, I have met one public and one school librarian who have had patrons that follow the tradition of Wica complain about the imbalance of most library books portraying witches as evil.

I have been warned at some schools not to mention ghosts or witches. I respect their requests because I have many other wonderful tales I can share, and the schools are paying for my services. At other schools I am told that the scarier and gorier my stories for older kids, the better. Then I roll up my mental sleeves and try to deliver the goods.

Disaster Preparedness

The title of this section was inspired by a bulletin board that listed how to behave in case of a natural disaster. Well, you are naturally going to have objections to your stories at some point whether you are a freelance performer or tell as part of another career.

1. Find out if the administration will stand by you and whether they have a procedure to handle complaints and an Arts Advocacy committee to defend you as an artist. If they don't, help them create such a procedure and form such a committee.

2. Decide whether you are willing to stand by your stories. Are they worth telling? Are they suitable for the audiences you are sharing them with? For example, upon examination you may choose to perform a violent Greek myth in a high school setting rather than with elementary students.

3. Support others in their battle against censorship. Don't wait until it happens to you. Get in touch with other people fighting censorship, and offer your support. To find out how you can help and to learn more about the problem, join the organizations listed in the "Resources" section at the end of the chapter.

4. Listen to the person's complaints without interrupting or becoming defensive or angry. Ask them to explain fully what their objections are. If you interrupt, you may be responding to an objection they are not making.

Sometimes, if you listen quietly you can defuse the situation.

5. If you think that you are being censored, document your situation. Share that information with the organizations listed in the "Resources" section. They may be able to offer suggestions or help. Tell everyone what has happened to you—the media, your arts council, the ACLU, other artists, and other listeners in the community. Ask for their support.

6. If possible, find the humor in the situation later to help reduce your stress. Jane Yolen, famous children's author and storyteller, has been called Satan's tool so often that she decided to choose which tool she is: a ball-peen hammer. She and her writing friends who have had similar problems created a T-shirt with the slogan: Satan's Tool Chest—The World Tour.

The Fearful Child

I once attended a workshop on children's personalities at a preschool conference. The workshop leader informed us that children have personalities from day one. The three categories she named were flexible, feisty, and fearful. The flexible child falls down and, if unhurt, gets up without crying. The feisty child may push other children down. The fearful child wails like a banshee and needs someone to pick her or him up off the floor. (These are, of course, simplifications.) If you wish to observe these three types in action, watch the "Rugrats" cartoon on the Nickelodeon television channel. Tommy is the flexible baby on the show. Chuckie is the fearful toddler, and Angelica is the feisty preschooler.

Those children are at every school assembly at which I tell. Luckily, the flexible children are in the majority.

A feisty kindergartner at the school where I was told that my stories would create nightmares demanded, "Tell Dracula!" This was at the time when horrific images from the movie

Dracula were being shown as previews on television shows that children watch.

But what about the fearful children? Many years ago one of them burst into tears and ran to her teacher as I told a Navajo tale in which Fox is dipped into a pot of boiling water. She didn't wait to hear that he was all right, just a little silly looking with all his fur boiled off.

After my experience at the school where I'd upset the PTA mother, I had hoped to be like storyteller Lee-Ellen Marvin and encourage schools to hire me for small-group tellings rather than for large assemblies. Then it would be easier to handle fearful children by explaining privately to each fearful listener that the tale is fiction and finding out exactly why the story bothered them. Because most schools I've performed at still prefer large assemblies, this has not always proved practical. I do sometimes end a spooky tale by asking the children at the assembly, "Did that story really happen?"

They shout, "No!"

Then I ask, "Is it a story?"

As they respond, "Yes!" I nod my head with a reassuring look on my face.

I have since discovered what I consider an important rule about spooky telling: the smaller the group, the scarier my stories seem. The same story that seems harmless when I am anchored behind a microphone in front of 200 students becomes more intense when 10 children are gathered around my chair and I twist my face to look like a witch and stare into their eyes.

Now, before I tell a story in which I take on frightening characterizations to a small group, I ask children who are under 10 if I am a witch, monster, cannibal, or whatever. After they reply in the negative, I remind them that we are pretending and that while I may pretend to be someone else in the next tale, I'm still just the storyteller. I also lighten my tone and notice which children have the widest eyes, are shrinking into themselves, or trying to pull in closer to another child or adult. I do not look at those children during the scary parts because a clown once told me that your eyes are laser beams to a fearful child. I also try to move physically away from those children during scary parts. As they see the other children responding in a brave, positive way to my story, it often empowers the frightened one to realize that we are playing and that nothing bad will actually happen.

Read the collections of spooky stories listed at the end of chapter 5 and try out your adaptations on the suggested age groups. You may find stories in each collection that could be used with other ages than what I've recommended. Whenever in doubt as to whether a story is too spooky for a particular age group, ask a few people who work with that age and perhaps try it out on a few flexible, fearful, and feisty children of that grade level.

Last Words

As you can see, telling stories professionally is not as easy as you perhaps thought. Yet it is still worth all the time, effort, and expense. I hope you will choose to tell stories not only professionally but legally and morally. To adapt the traditional actor's good luck wish, "Break a leg," I say to all of you, "Bite your tongue!"

Resources

Aids for Multicultural Research

Culturegrams
Brigham Young University
David M. Kennedy Center for International
    Studies
Publication Services
280 H RCB
Provo, Utah 84602
    These are handy reference sheets about
    different countries.

Organizations Fighting Censorship

Censorship Committee of the American
    Library Association
American Library Association
50 East Huron Street
Chicago, IL 60611
Ph: 312-944-6780
    Write for their pamphlets and guidelines
    about techniques for protecting freedom
    of speech, such as the Library Bill of
    Rights.

Midwest Center for Arts, Entertainment and
    the Law
c/o Dan Tyson
100 S. 5th Street
Minneapolis, MN 55402
Ph: 612-332-1030

National Campaign for Freedom of Expression
P.O. Box 21465
Seattle, WA 98111
Write for their packet.

People for the American Way
2000 M Street NW, #400
Washington, D.C. 20036
Ph: 202-467-4999
Write for their ARTS SAVE handbook.

Further Reading

Stories from Different Cultures

There are so many stories from so many cultures to choose from! This list is just a tiny start. Find the cultures you are drawn to or come from, and keep searching for more information.

Caduto, Michael J., and Joseph Bruchac. *Keepers of Life: Discovering Plants Through Native American Stories and Earth Activities for Children.* Golden, CO: Fulcrum, 1994.
Joseph Bruchac is of Abenaki ancestry, and all of his books of Native American stories are recommended.

Coburn, Jewell Reinhart, and Van Quyen Duong. *Beyond the East Wind: Legends and Folktales of Vietnam.* Thousand Oaks, CA: Burn, Hart, 1976.

Cohen, Hennig, and Tristram Potter Coffin, eds. *The Folklore of American Holidays: A Compilation of More Than 500 Beliefs, Legends, Superstitions, Proverbs, Riddles, Poems, Songs, Dances, Games, Plays, Pageants, Fairs, Foods, and Processions Associated with Over 120 American Calendar Customs and Festivals.* 2d ed. Detroit: Gale, 1991.

Creeden, Sharon. *Fair Is Fair: World Folktales of Justice.* Little Rock, AR: August House, 1994.
Actual cases, laws, and commentary are included along with tales from Burma, Morocco, Majorca, and other places.

Cunningham, Keith. *American Indians' Kitchen-Table Stories: Contemporary Conversations with Cherokee, Sioux, Hopi, Osage, Navajo, Zuni, and Members of Other Nations.* Little Rock, AR: August House, 1992.

Dailey, Sheila. *Putting the World in a Nutshell: The Art of the Formula Tale.* Bronx, NY: H. W. Wilson, 1994.

Faulkner, William J. *The Days When the Animals Talked: Black American Folktales and How They Came to Be.* Chicago: Follett, 1977.

Forest, Heather. *Wonder Tales from Around the World.* Little Rock, AR: August House, 1995.

Gail, Judy, and Linda A. Houlding. *Day of the Moon Shadow: Tales with Ancient Answers to Scientific Questions.* Englewood, CO: Libraries Unlimited, 1995.
Siksika (Blackfoot) Indian, Peruvian, Aboriginal Australian, and other cultures have explained such natural phenomena as why the dinosaurs died and where birds songs came from. This book gives background information on the cultures and the science, the stories, and songs and explains how the authors came to write six entirely original tales for the book in addition to the eight that are based more closely on folklore.

Geisler, Harlynne. "African Storytelling." *Story Bag Newsletter* (February/March 1992): 5.

———. "A Conversation with David Whitehorse." *Story Bag Newsletter* (December 1989): 2.

———. "History Is Full of Emotion, Fun, and Children." *Story Bag Newsletter* (June/July 1991) 1–3.

Graham, Gail. *The Beggar in the Blanket and Other Vietnamese Tales.* New York: Dial Press, 1970.

Haddawy, Husain, trans. *The Arabian Nights II: Sinbad and Other Popular Stories.* New York: W. W. Norton, 1995.

Haddawy was born in Baghdad and presents stories such as "Ala al-Din" ("Aladdin") as well as an introduction that traces their history. Don't let Disney be your only source for these fabulous tales!

Johnson, Charles, ed. *Myths, Legends, and Folk Tales from the Hmong of Laos: With Explanatory Notes on Hmong Culture, Customs, and Beliefs.* St. Paul, MN: Linguistics Department, Macalester College, 1985.
In English and Hmong.

Lankford, George E., ed. *Native American Legends: The Southeastern Tribes.* Little Rock, AR: August House, 1993.

Lester, Julius. *The Tales of Uncle Remus: The Adventures of B'rer Rabbit, Volume 1, as Told by Julius Lester.* New York: Dial Books, 1987.

Livo, Lauren J., Glenn McGlathery, and Norma J. Livo. *Of Bugs and Beasts: Fact, Folklore, and Activities.* Englewood, CO: Libraries Unlimited, 1995.

Leeches, clams, razorback suckers, slugs, and unappealing animals are found in folklore of Native American, African-American, Asian, and other cultures. The stories are followed up by extensive information and activities about the animals.

Livo, Norma J., and Dia Cha. *Folk Stories of the Hmong: Peoples of Laos, Thailand and Vietnam.* Englewood, CO: Libraries Unlimited, 1991.

MacDonald, Margaret Read. *Celebrate the World: Twenty Tellable Folktales for Multicultural Festivals.* Bronx, NY: H. W. Wilson, 1994.

Malpezzi, Frances M., and William M. Clements. *Italian-American Folklore: Proverbs, Songs, Games, Folktales, Foodways, Superstitions, Folk Remedies, and More.* Little Rock, AR: August House, 1993.

McNeil, Heather. *Hyena and the Moon: Stories to Tell from Kenya.* Englewood, CO: Libraries Unlimited, 1993.

This white American has gone to Kenya and collected these tales in a way that shows a lot of respect for the cultures she finds. She includes information on the different groups that tell the stories and gives tips on telling. An audiocassette of her reciting the stories is also available.

Pellowski, Anne. *The World of Storytelling.* Bronx, NY: H. W. Wilson, 1990.

Pelton, Mary Helen, and Jacqueline DiGennaro. *Images of a People: Tlingit Myths and Legends.* Englewood, CO: Libraries Unlimited, 1992.

Reneaux, J. J. *Cajun Folktales.* Little Rock, AR: August House, 1992.

Schram, Peninnah, ed. *Chosen Tales: Stories Told by Jewish Storytellers.* Northvale, NJ: Jason Aronson, 1995.

———. *Jewish Stories One Generation Tells Another.* Northvale, NJ: Jason Aronson, 1987.

Sheehan, Ethna. *Folk and Fairy Tales from Around the World.* New York: Dodd, 1970.

Sherman, Josepha. *Once upon a Galaxy.* Little Rock, AR: August House, 1994.

The original tales behind contemporary science fiction books, cartoons, films, and television shows are given with explanatory notes.

Sierra, Judy. *Cinderella.* Phoenix, AZ: Oryx Press, 1992.

See all of the Oryx Multicultural Folktale series for many versions of familiar folktales with notes explaining cultural background of each version. This includes "Hansel and Gretel," "Beauties & Beasts," "Tom Thumb," and "A Knock at the Door," which is a collection of folktales about the dangerous character who knocks at the door.

Spagnoli, Cathy. "Storytelling in China and Japan." *Story Bag Newsletter* (August 1989): 3–4.

———. "Telling in Japan Today." *Story Bag Newsletter* (August/September 1992): 3–4.

———. *Thao Kham, the Pebble Shooter: A Tale from Laos.* Bothell, WA: Wright Group, 1995.
See all of Spagnoli's picture books in the Tall Tales and Tricksters from Asia series available from the Wright Group.

Swann, Brian. *Smoothing the Ground: Essays on the Native American Oral Tradition.* Berkeley, CA: University of California Press, 1983.

Tyler, Royall, ed. *Japanese Tales.* New York: Pantheon Books, 1987.
See all the volumes in Pantheon's Fairy Tale and Folklore Library for unusual collections with excellent source notes.

Vathanaprida, Supaporn. *Thai Tales: Folktales of Thailand.* Englewood, CO: Libraries Unlimited, 1994.

Vigil, Angel. *The Corn Woman: Stories and Legends of the Hispanic Southwest.* Englewood, CO: Libraries Unlimited, 1994.

West, John O. *Mexican-American Folklore.* Little Rock, AR: August House, 1988.

Wilhelm, Robert Bela. "Storytelling: Morality or Imagination in Religion?" *Story Bag Newsletter* (August/September 1992): 1–4.

The Roles of Women in Fairy Tales

Bettelheim, Bruno. *The Uses of Enchantment: The Meaning and Importance of Fairy Tales.* New York: Vintage Books, 1976.

Jongeward, Dorothy, and Dru Scott. *Women as Winners: Transactional Analysis for Personal Growth.* Reading, MA: Addison-Wesley, 1976.

National Women's History Project catalog, 7738 Bell Road, Windsor, CA 95492-8518.

Sale, Roger. *Fairy Tales and After: From Snow White to E. B. White.* Cambridge, MA: Harvard University, 1978.

Stone, Kay. "Marchen to Fairytale: An Unmagical Transformation." *Western Folklore* 40 (July 1981): 232–44.

———. "Things Walt Disney Never Told Us." *Journal of American Folklore* 88 (January 1975): 42–50.

Zipes, Jack. *Breaking the Magic Spell.* Austin, TX: University of Texas Press, 1979.

———, ed. *Don't Bet on the Prince: Contemporary Feminist Fairy Tales in North America and England.* New York: Methuen, 1986.

Story Collections Featuring Strong Women and Gentle Men

Barchers, Suzanne. *Wise Women; Folk and Fairy Tales from Around the World.* Englewood, CO: Libraries Unlimited, 1990.

Carter, Angela. *The Old Wives Fairy Tale Book.* New York: Pantheon Books, 1990. Not all stories are suitable for children.

Haven, Kendall F. *Amazing American Women: 40 Fascinating 5-Minute Reads.* Englewood, CO: Libraries Unlimited, 1995.

Lurie, Alison. *Clever Gretchen and Other Forgotten Folktales.* New York: Thomas Y. Crowell, 1980.

McCarty, Toni. *The Skull in the Snow and Other Folktales.* Boston: Houghton Mifflin, 1975.

Minard, Rosemary. *Womenfolk and Fairy Tales.* Boston: Houghton Mifflin, 1975.

Phelps, Ethel Johnston. *The Maid of the North: Feminist Folk Tales from Around the World.* New York: Holt, Rinehart & Winston, 1981.

———. *Tatterhood and Other Tales: Stories of Magic and Adventure*. New York: Feminist Press, 1978.

Censorship and Storytelling

"Defending the Story." In *The Storyteller's Start-Up Book: Finding, Learning, Performing and Using Folktales*. Edited by Margaret Read MacDonald. Little Rock, AR: August House, 1993.

Grimm, Jacob, and Wilhelm Grimm. "Little Red-Cap." In *Grimms Household Tales*. Translated and edited by Margaret Hunt. London: George Bell and Sons, 1884. Re-issue, Detroit: Singing Tree Press, 1968.

Hofer, Marie. "The Thrill of Fear." *Storytelling Magazine* (Fall 1990): 9–12.

"Little Red Riding Hood." In *The Uses of Enchantment: The Meaning and Importance of Fairy Tales*. Edited by Bruno Bettelheim. New York: Vintage Books, 1976

Livo, Norma J. *Who's Afraid...? Facing Children's Fears with Folktales*. Englewood, CO: Libraries Unlimited, 1994.

Perrault, Charles. "Little Red Riding Hood." In *The Blue Fairy Book*. Edited by Andrew Lang. New York: Dover, 1889, 1965.

"A Second Gaze at Little Red Riding Hood's Trials and Tribulations." In *Don't Bet on the Prince: Contemporary Feminist Fairy Tales in North America and England*. Edited by Jack Zipes. New York: Methuen, 1986.

Werner, Craig. "The Wolf Speaks Out." *The Story Bag Newsletter* (November 1988): 3.

Zipes, Jack. *The Trials and Tribulations of Little Red Riding Hood: Versions of the Tale in Sociocultural Context*. Portsmouth, NH: Heinemann, 1983.

Telling Multicultural Tales

"Delicious Shivers: Spooky Stories." *Story Bag: A National Storytelling Newsletter* (1994), 5361 Javier St., San Diego, CA 92117-3215, 1994.

This packet has the full texts of seven funny and scary stories for children, teens, and adults; information on the multicultural aspects of the bogeyman; advice from Nancy Duncan on how to handle censorship problems; and storytellers' experiences with complaints about traditional folktales. Send $5.50 to cover the cost of photocopying and mailing to *Story Bag: A National Storytelling Newsletter*.

Hall, Edward T. *The Hidden Dimension*. Magnolia, MA: Peter Smith, 1992.

———. *The Silent Language*. New York: Doubleday, 1959.

Jackson, Stevan, and Dianne Hackworth. "Stories in Public Domain: Removing the Mystery." *Story Bag Newsletter* (February/March 1993): 5–6.

An important article that tells you how to find out what is copyrighted and what is now in public domain and can be used without asking permission. You can also call 1-800-444-4302, the Copyright Hot Line run by the Association for Information Media and Equipment.

Murray, Wendy. "How to Choose the Best Multicultural Books." *Instructor Magazine* (November/December 1995): 46–53.

Provides some guidelines for selecting and presenting stories from Asian, Jewish, African American, Native American, and Latino cultures. It also includes an annotated bibliography of 10 recommended books about each culture and lists other authors who write about the cultures with knowledge and respect.

Norwick, Kenneth, and Jerry Chasen. *The Rights of Authors, Artists, and Other Creative People: The Basic ACLU Guide to Author and Artist Rights*. 2d. ed. Carbondale, IL: Southern Illinois University Press, 1992.

Appendix A

Hire the Pros

How to Host a Freelance Storyteller at Your School or Library

To speak is to sow; to listen is to reap.
—Turkish proverb

One of the saddest conversations I ever overheard was between my nine-year-old niece Monica and her great-grandfather. She asked him to tell her a story, and this man—who could recount with relish his funny and hair-raising adventures on the Yangtze River in the 1920s—replied, "I'm not a storyteller; Harlynne is." Of course, I hastened to tell him what I hope you already know: "You don't have to be a paid performer to be a story-teller." Every human is a storyteller, just as every human is a singer. The fact that there are opera singers in the world shouldn't keep you from singing a lullaby to your baby or joining in on "Row, Row, Row Your Boat" with the children under your care.

Even if you choose to bring in profession-als, let the children know that they should value the natural tellers within their family and community. You can bring in these folk-tale tellers to share oral history and folklore, or you might have children tape family members telling stories in their first language, which the children then translate for the rest of the group. Len Cabral, a Rhode Island storyteller, does this so that the children will understand that their families are full of storytellers and be proud of their first language. If you do bring folk tellers to your school or library, ask them how they would be most comfortable in presenting their stories. Many will prefer a small group of listeners to an auditorium filled with people.

Still, there may be times when you wish to host the storytelling equivalents of folk musicians or rock stars. Freelance storytellers have devoted their time and energy to stories. They can provide both expertise and artistry to your school or library.

This appendix can be rewritten and distributed to potential bookers.

What Is a Storyteller?

Storyteller is a hot word these days, and many entertainers are using it to describe themselves. It may not matter to you if the entertainer you hire uses a combination of puppetry, oral interpretation, acting, dance, reader's theater, creative dramatics, clowning, singing, magic, or other performance skills as long as what they do is appropriate, educational, and entertaining.

But if you have decided that you want a particular style of storytelling, don't assume that all storytellers will deliver what you want. Try to see them in action and ask specific questions about what their show is all about before hiring them. You might also ask for references. It can save you both from unpleasant surprises.

Also be aware that a great performer may not necessarily be a great teacher and vice versa. You may choose to use different storytellers on stage than the ones you choose to teach their art in the classroom or library.

Money

Chapter 9 tells you the freelance teller's financial considerations and in the section "Where Will They Find Money to Pay You?" offers suggestions for sources of funds you might use to hire a performer.

If you know of a storyteller who is coming to your area for a festival or concert, arrange to have them visit your library or school. It can save you the cost of a plane ticket because the travel expenses will have already been paid by the other bookers.

Where Do You Find Storytellers?

There are a variety of ways to locate a storyteller for your particular program:

1. Ask members of your staff and parents if they've heard any tellers they would recommend.

2. Ask the children's librarians at your public library.

3. Ask your local storytellers' guild, or get in touch with the National Storytelling Association. They have a *National Storytelling Directory* available for a small charge but will gladly tell you of tellers and storytelling groups in your area. If you decide to use storytellers from other places, you may have to pay travel costs, room, and board.

4. Check local parenting magazines for ads or articles about storytellers.

5. Attend storytelling festivals, conferences, and concerts. NSA, *Story Bag: A National Storytelling Newsletter*, and other storytelling newsletters can inform you about such events.

6. Attend storytelling concerts or workshops at educational and library conferences.

7. Ask other performers. Puppeteers, magicians, actors, clowns, and musicians often know storytellers.

Questions to Ask Before Hiring

You want to get the best performer for your money. Asking these questions will help assure that outcome.

1. What experience do you have as a storyteller in libraries or schools?

2. How many years have you been telling in libraries or schools?

3. Can you give me any references from libraries or schools in my area or elsewhere?

4. What do you charge? (Only ask this after explaining exactly what you are hiring the teller for, as this will make a difference in the fee.)

5. Can you send me a brochure or other information?

6. Where can I hear you tell? (Whenever possible, go see the performer in action.)

7. Do you have a tape of stories I could buy? (If you aren't able to see the teller at a show, then listening to a tape can give you some idea of what he or she will be like in person.)

8. Are you able to tell stories on a particular subject? (Seventh-grade teachers might want Greek myths; a school with a large Hispanic population might ask for tales from Mexico; leprechaun stories could be a delight on March 17, and so on.)

When calling to book a teller, first identify yourself, your position, and your school or library. If you are looking for a storyteller for a specific occasion, story topic, date, or age level, state this near the beginning of the conversation. If unable to fulfill your requirements, the performer may be able to suggest someone who can.

Questions to Ask
Once You've Hired a Storyteller

1. Does the teller have any special requirements, such as a microphone on a stand, a glass of water, children seated in rows on the floor, blackboard, and so on?

2. Do you need to provide the teller with lunch? If so, are there any dietary restrictions to be aware of?

3. How long is each presentation (assembly, classroom lecture, etc.)? Let the artist know if she or he must stick exactly to the time allotted or if it's all right to run over by a few minutes.

4. How much time is needed between presentations?

5. How many presentations is the person willing to do in a day?

6. Is there an introduction the teller wants you to read, or special things the artist would like you to say during your own introduction?

7. How many breaks does the teller need?

8. May the presentation be taped? (Never spring this request at the last minute. Always ask in advance if you plan to tape a presentation. Some tellers will have to turn you down due to copyright restrictions.)

9. Does the teller have a contract you need to sign? (If the teller doesn't, send him or her a confirmation letter clearly providing directions to the location of the site, its address and phone number, the name of the person in charge, dates and times of all presentations, specific details on what the teller is hired to do, and what your obligations are, such as providing a

hand-held microphone or copying handouts. Never change the schedule or any details without informing the performer in advance. Also notify the storyteller if invoices need to be sent and to what staff person and address.)

Be sure to alert the storyteller to any situations or story topics that can cause problems. Perhaps there has been a recent death of some-

one close to your school or library community. I was at one school the day after a student committed suicide and at another school the morning after a mother died in a car crash. I have certain stories that I tell that involve death. I did not consider those narratives appropriate for those school populations on those days. I was so glad that in both cases staff members informed me of the local tragedies.

Preparing Your Library or School for a Storytelling Experience

Let all staff members know that a storyteller is coming. Even though the teller will choose children's stories for an assembly, adults will find themselves just as involved. Good literature is meant to be heard by all ages, and the idea that folktales were only meant for children is a fairly recent (and wrong) one. Very definitely the library, reading, administrative, and mental health staff should be invited, but if at all possible give janitorial, secretarial, and kitchen staff a chance to listen. They deserve stories as much as anyone. If the students see that adults from all over the school have stopped their work to listen, they will realize that stories are important.

Tactfully suggest to the staff that it is not appropriate to grade homework or talk during the presentation. (At one school I had a teacher hide a colleague's newspaper so that he couldn't work on the crossword puzzle as he had done so blatantly and rudely during my first student workshop.)

Also, suggest to your staff that the students look to them to model enthusiasm and interest. Nothing is more disturbing to me than noticing that while the children and I are pretending to be roosters flapping our wings, some of the teachers are sitting with their arms crossed.

Ask the staff to seat near themselves any children who might misbehave so they can handle the problem unobtrusively and that they discuss appropriate listening behavior with their classes. This includes sitting quietly unless directed by the storyteller to participate and applauding at the end of each story.

Prepare the location where the teller will be situated by making sure that the area has been straightened up, that the floor has been swept or vacuumed, and that any visual or auditory distractions are removed. If there is an intercom or speaker to the office, turn it off if possible. Nothing jerks the listeners out of their story trance faster than a metallic voice reminding them that milk money is due today.

In a library setting, notice if there is a drinking fountain or photocopying machine near the performance area. If so, unplug the drinking fountain if it has a noisy engine and put a sign on the photocopying machine that it is out of order and cannot be used during the story hour. If the checkout desk is near the storytelling area, ask your staff to speak softly, and ask patrons who are checking out to speak softly too. If at all possible, designate a staff member to handle problems during the story hour.

Preparing Students
for a Storytelling Experience

Use the "Preparing Students for a Storytelling Experience" handout in chapter 3 to help students get ready to enjoy and understand the show or workshop.

Meet the Storyteller Halfway

Chapter 12 details some of the challenges tellers encounter in schools and libraries. A little foresight could have prevented many of those sticky situations. Preparing your listeners, staff, and story area will be a big help. You can also be a good host to your guest by taking care of the following points. If you are too busy to handle these activities, find other staff or volunteers to help.

1. Sound Equipment

    Test the equipment a week before the storyteller's visit so that there is time to fix any problems, borrow or rent another system, or notify the storyteller to bring his or her own equipment. Test the sound system again the day before the visit.

    Make sure that the person in charge of setting the system up the day of the show has been reminded of the time the equipment must be ready and of the performer's requirements (such as a clip-on microphone, etc.). If at all possible, this person should stay through at least the first presentation in case of problems.

2. Welcoming the Storyteller

    At one school I was actually welcomed in the crowded parking lot by a sign with my name on it reserving a parking space for me! Little touches like that mean a lot. A sign made and decorated by the children can be posted in the performance space.

    A person should be delegated to meet the performer in the office, welcome him or her, lead the way to the performance room, point out restrooms and the staff lounge, make sure the sound equipment is ready, help unload the car, notify the teller when it is time to start each show, introduce other staff members, and act as the emcee.

3. Saying Thanks

    The few times that I have been surprised at the end of a show with a gift of fresh flowers or at lunch time with a meal at a nice restaurant courtesy of the library or PTA have been special to me.

    I love to read the comments and to look at the darling pictures that children often send me a few days after my visit. The one thank-you letter still up on my bulletin board after two years is a poster sent from a kindergarten. The teacher had written a short thank-you note in large letters, and all the children had signed their names. Then each child had drawn a character from one of my stories around the border of the poster.

    Those letters written on official stationary that mention specific things that the listeners and staff enjoyed and learned from the presentations—including feedback on how to improve the storyteller's performance—are very useful.

    An excellent way to say thanks to a good teller is to recommend them to other libraries or schools. That way you support the artist and the art.

    Don't forget to hire the teller again next year. Most have several shows and workshops you can choose from for an encore.

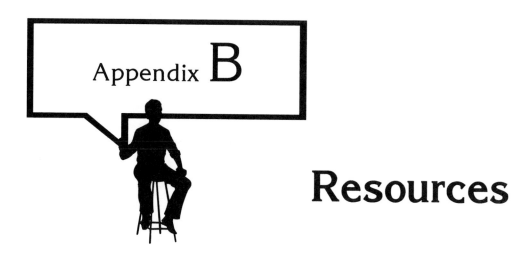

Appendix B

Resources

The following is a list of resources you can contact to find potential clients, locate booking conventions, and find performance organizations.

Mailing List Companies

You can buy mailing lists of potential clients and audiences from specialized companies who sell address lists for bookstores, schools, libraries, clubs, religious institutions, social service groups, and so on. Each company has a catalog that lists hundreds of mailing lists to choose from. The lists can be limited based on state or zip code. For an extra charge, the lists can be printed on mailing labels. These are two companies that have sent me catalogs:

American List Council, Inc.
88 Orchard Road CN-5219
Princeton, NJ 08543
Ph: 800-ALC-LIST
Fax: 908-874-4433

PCS Mailing List Company
85 Constitution Lane
Danvers, MA 01923
Ph: 800-532-LIST
Fax: 508-777-9161

Booking Conferences

Artists as well as presenters may belong to these organizations.

Association of Performing Arts Presenters
1112 16th Street NW, Suite 400
Washington, DC 20036
Ph: 202-833-2787
Fax: 202-833-1543
Conference is held annually in New York City. Association also published a magazine and keeps a database. You can also purchase from the association *Words That*

Sell, a book by Richard Bayan that teaches you how to word headlines, describe free offers, justify prices, and so on.

National Showcase
Carole Sullivan, Chair
Kennedy Center
Washington, DC 20566
Ph: 202-872-1500
Toll free: 800-228-9290

National Showcase of Performing Arts for
  Children
Performing Arts for Children
1 Allegheny Square, Suite 245
Pittsburgh, PA 15212

International Society of Performing Arts
  Administrators
4920 Plainfield NE, Suite 3
Grand Rapids, MI 49505
Ph: 616-364-3000
Fax: 616-364-9010
  Annual conference in December in New
  York. Annual conference in June moves
  to sites around the world.

Annual Regional Booking Conferences

ACUCCA
6225 University Avenue
Madison, WI 53705-1009
Ph: 608-233-7400
  Midwestern showcase for university,
  schools, and community concerts.

Arts Northwest
P.O. Box 55877
Seattle, WA 98155
Ph: 206-365-4143
Fax: 206-365-8618
  Booking conferences are held in Wash-
  ington, Oregon, or Idaho.

Center East for the Arts Showcase
Jo Ann O'Brien
7701 Lincoln Avenue
Skokie, IL 60077
Ph: 312-673-6305
  Midwestern bookers.

Southern Children's Theatre Showcase
c/o Civic Theatre for Young People
1001 East Princeton Street
Orlando, FL 32803

Southern Children's Theatre Circuit
Mary W. Wood
302 Hillcrest Drive
High Point, NC 27262
Ph: 919-882-2347

Southwest Arts Conference
c/o Mollie Lakin-Hayes
417 West Roosevelt
Phoenix, AZ 85003
Ph: 602-255-5884
  Held in conjunction with Scottsdale Center for the Arts Festival.

Western Alliance of Arts Administrators
44 Page Street, Suite #604B
San Francisco, CA 94102
Ph: 415-621-4400
Fax: 415-621-2533

For a list of smaller showcases in New York,
  New England, the South, and the East,
  write Chris Holder, *Artists with Class*, 66
  Jenkins Road, Burnt Hills, NY 12027.

Canadian Booking Conferences

Showcase
Robert Monteith, Theatre Manager
Cleary International Center
201 Riverside Drive West
Windsor, ON N9A 5K4

Vancouver Children's Festival Showcase
Marjorie Maclean, Director of Programming
302/601 Cambie Street
Vancouver, BC V6B 2P1

Arts Agencies

National Assembly of State Arts Organizations
1010 Vermont Avenue NW, Suite 920
Washington, DC 20005
      Write them for a listing of state arts agencies.

National Headquarters
of Organizations

American Business Women's Association
127 West 24th Street
New York, NY 10011-1914
Ph: 212-645-0770

American Library Association
50 East Huron Street
Chicago, IL 60611
Ph: 312-944-6780

Business Network International
268 South Bucknell Avenue
Claremont, CA 91711-4907
Ph: 909-624-2227
Toll free: 800-825-8286
Fax: 909-625-9671

Chamber of Commerce of the U.S.
1615 H Street NW
Washington, DC 20062
Ph: 202-659-6000

Clowns of America
P.O. Box 570
Lake Jackson, TX 77566-0570
Ph: 409-297-6699

International Brotherhood of Magicians
P.O. Box 89
Bluffton, OH 45817
Ph: 419-358-8555

International Listening Association
c/o Dr. Charles Roberts
Box 90340
McNeese State University
Lake Charles, LA 70609
Ph: 318-475-5120

International Reading Association
P.O. Box 8139
Newark, DE 19714-8139
Ph: 302-731-1600

Jaycees
P.O. Box 7
Tulsa, OK 74121
Ph: 918-584-2481

National Association of Women Business
      Owners
221 North LaSalle Street, Suite 2026
Chicago, IL 60601
Ph: 312-922-0465

National Chamber of Commerce for Women
10 Waterside Plaza, Suite 6H
New York, NY 10010
Ph: 212-685-3454

National Council of Teachers of English
1111 Kenyon Road
Urbana, IL 61801
Ph: 217-328-3870

National Education Association
1201 16th Street NW
Washington, DC 20036
Ph: 202-833-4000

National Federation of Business and Profes-
      sional Women's Clubs
2012 Massachusetts Avenue NW
Washington, DC 20036
Ph: 202-293-1100

National Story League
c/o Elizabeth Raabe
52 Stephen F. Austin
Conroe, TX 77302
Ph: 409-273-5100

National Storytelling Association
P.O. Box 309
Jonesborough, TN 37659
Ph: 615-753-2171
        Toll free: 800-525-4514

North American Folk Music and Dance
        Alliance
P.O. Box 5010
Chapel Hill, NC 27514
Ph: 919-962-3397
Fax: 919-962-4453
E-mail: 70632.3264@compuserve.com

Puppeteers of America
5 Cricklewood Path
Pasadena, CA 91107
Ph: 818-797-5748

Society of American Magicians
P.O. Box 290068
St. Louis, MO 63129
Ph: 314-846-5659

Whole Language Umbrella
P.O. Box 2029
Bloomington, IN 47402-2029
Ph: 812-856-8280
Fax: 812-856-8287

Index

About the Author

Harlynne Geisler has an English Secondary Education degree and a Master's degree in Library Science from the University of Illinois. In 1980, after 14 years as a school and public librarian, Harlynne changed her career focus to become a freelance professional storyteller. She has taught storytelling to clowns, magicians, teachers, children, college students, parents, puppeteers, librarians, and storytellers in six states. Harlynne has performed across North America in such diverse places as New York, Canada, Texas, New Mexico, and California.

Harlynne is the editor of *Story Bag: A National Storytelling Newsletter* and is a columnist for *Laugh Makers Magazine*. She has published more than 150 articles in 30 publications, including *Storytelling Magazine*.

She founded and directed the Storytellers of San Diego from 1981 to 1985. She is a member of the National Storytelling Association, the International Reading Association, and the Whole Language Umbrella, as well as founder and organizer of the Southern California Storyswapping Festival, 1984–1985.